A Beautiful Resistance

Everything We Already Are

Our Deepest Thanks

Our first issue of A Beautiful Resistance would have been impossible without the generous help of Hecate Demetersdatter and Peter Dybing.

In addition, the cover art was funded by Jes Minah

This first issue is printed in color thanks to the support of Jeremy Real

Also, we'd like to thank George Caffentzis and Jeremy Real for their additional donations

Additionally, Gods&Radicals would like to thank our initial Supporters:

Soli	Violet Fortuna
Dizzy Wizard	Stan the Man
Darkmoonshining	Petery Dybing
Katherine Heigh	Rick Hobbs
Tony Rella	Brian Rosian
Niki Whiting	John Halstead
Patricia Awen Fey O'Luanaigh	Scott-Richardson-Read
Terence P. Ward	Rhiannon Theurer
Jonathan Levy	Anonymous
Andrew M. Reichart	Charlotte Ruddick
Andrew Thrift	Anonymous

The Editor would like particularly to thank
those who support him via Patreon,
without whom the time to edit, compile,
and distribute this journal would have been impossible.
Also, deep thanks to his Lionheart.

Additional thanks to Alley Valkyrie, Syren Nagakyrie, and Lisha Sterling,
to Peter Grey for inspiring the whole thing,,
Anne Newkirk Niven for all her helpful advice, and
all the revolutionary dead,
and the gods of liberation.

Foreword

We are the generation that does not act, that has outsourced our thinking to search engines. We have been bought by the small pleasures of conformity and consumption, whilst being rendered into a precariat, too risk averse to revolt. Debt bows us over our mobile phones, whilst we are stupefied by drone deliveries that bring us objects that cannot match our desires but are made from the resources that our species' survival depends upon.

We have been told that magic is not political and that we should seek acceptance at whatever cost, whilst our rulers openly use state ritual and confiscate the possessions of those who curse corporations and the bodies of those who engage in the rites of resistance. We have been told that witchcraft is not class struggle, though it reverses the flow of state violence. We have been told that spirit is an illusion, despite the proof of it down to a quantum level. We are even told by our own cadres, in thrall to materialism, that radicals cannot believe in gods or spiritual creatures. But it is not that we *believe*, it is that these are our lived experiences and that we are compelled by them to act. Religion is used to bind, but none can bind the throng of voices that speak to us, through us, which cannot be medicalised as opium dream, madness, or sheer hysteria.

Even the most ardent materialists are haunted by digital ghosts, ever hungry; they demand to be fed. These translucent skeins are braided into lives that exist in the hinterland of a dead space. It is not they that follow us, but we who are drawn on by our own dazzling shadows. Contritely smiling we go contorting after our own images. We cannot seem to exorcise the product that claims to be us, that wears what we recognise- with horror - to be our own face.

As the digital engulfs us in the internet of things, there will be less cropmarks, less filters; we go straight to digital without a feedback loop being required. Our ghosts become ever more monstrous, our frailty exposed in high definition. These are the ghosts that must be laid to rest in order that we can encounter the presence of spirits. We need to create a space to dream in, rather than allowing our experiences to be simultaneously overwritten by the banal messages of commerce and conformity. Poetry is one such space, ritual is another. I can see the fault line exactly here: the desire of this generation is not (as the dead traditionally ask) to be remembered, but to be forgotten. Our need to reclaim anonymity is mistaken for shrinking into a hoody, for not engaging. We want the ghost to stop making demands and to be erased from the timeline. When the servers burn and the cameras smash, the youth will rejoice; it is only the old who are digital hoarders.

So I will make a prediction: the internet will be silently abandoned as it becomes brought entirely within the control of the corporations. The enclosure of the digital commons will dispossess it of all meaning. Just as television became anathema in the eighties, so will digital media within ten years, perhaps sooner, and it is this generation that will reject it first, as their avenues of retreat and free communication are systematically blocked. Radicals take heart! Control is ultimately self-defeating entropy. Belief in neoliberal absolutism is failing, as it cannot keep the promise of a middleclass lifestyle for all. Climate collapse will break the supply lines of affluence. There will be no reason not to fight back for the generation that sees we are gone into the smeared penumbra of dusk, those to whom no further promises can be made, to whom the gods speak. As the new poor, witchcraft is our last resource: a witchcraft that does not wait for the gears of history to turn, but acts freely in all the worlds.

Do not underestimate the strength that this publication evinces. We confound expectations. *Gods and Radicals* is a defining publication that marks a new moment in magic, witchcraft and paganism; the moment when we remember our history, our ancestry, our land and our bodies. Story is not an end in itself but becomes ritual action embedded in place. The land speaks through us, we will not let our voices and bodies be co-opted by the nation, nor the corporate state. Our voices are diverse, and though despair and anger may mark our awakening, it is love that unites us.

Peter Grey

Is the co-founder of Scarlet Imprint, and the author of Apocalyptic Witchcraft

Everything We Already Are

An introduction

Rhyd Wildermuth

Y**ou've heard the clamour, I am certain.** The pain. The fear. The torment of acidic oceans rising, the sorrow of ancient forests dying. The wails of refugees fleeing resource wars, the lonely lament of the last White Rhinos and Eastern Cougars. Costs and temperatures rising as more wells are drilled to stave off droughts of water and fuel, panic masked as progress against the terror of a world that doesn't work any longer.

This is the moan of the machine, William Blake's 'satanic mill,' the gears of Capital slipping in its thirst to grind bone, stone, and soul. Forest into lumber, land into property, human into worker, art into commodity, life into profit: they found the Philosopher's Stone, and Nature has become the base metal to be transmuted into their gold.

Shelves in pale-lit store-houses sell our world back to us. Tin cans of processed bounty, plastic trinkets spun from polymeric threads, tiny windows onto the memory of community, culture, meaning. We thumb and scroll through images of friends we never see, liking what they had for dinner while eating meals we didn't have time to cook. We have become the Lady of Shalott staring into enchanted mirrors, despairing to look out of our lightning-struck towers.

But despair is the shadow of hope, its amorous twin. Sorrow and joy, desire and fear, birth and death—each is nothing without its Other, and only together become something new. The mystery of the Divine Twins is the mystery of the dialectic—the Romanticists who restored the Pagan to the West fought the same war as Marx against the new occulted Authority.

As Silvia Federici has shown, the slaughter of witches made way for the enchainment of the worker—and witches don't stay dead. Bearing hammers, led by a ghostly King, the Luddites sought to sabotage the machine. Dressed in drag, the Whitboys and Molly McGuires, the Levelers and Rebeccas issued eviction notices in the name of divine queens and ancient crones. In Bois Caiman, priests bled vows to Erzulie against their imperial masters. The Haymarket Massacre is celebrated on Beltane. In the salons and bedrooms of Oscar Wilde and Edward Carpenter were the anarchists and the occultists, dreaming lustily of revolution. The pagan resurgence soaked the sweat-drenched bodies of hippies and revolutionaries in the 60's. Amongst puppets and tear gas, witches invoked circle and goddess against global capitalism.

What you hold in your hands is nothing new, and it's yours. It's what you've always held in your hands, be you witch or academic or punk, artist or mage or druid, worker or heathen or poet. *It's your inheritance.* Through one hand courses a river of power, the dreams of the poor, the revolt of the enslaved, the desire of the forests, the hope of birth. Through the other flows streams of wisdom, frantic scribblings of philosopher, guiding spirits of dying earth, crumbling leaf of herb and grimoire, echoing prayer of the tortured heretic.

We are heirs to magic. We are heirs to revolution. We are heirs to dream.

A Beautiful Resistance is a tapestry woven from threads of hope and despair, desire and fear, sorrow and joy. It's the words of 28 writers and works of three artists, a dream conceived from a longing, a search for what we've always known to be true. We are those who have always existed, initiates of a revolutionary current, citizens of an Other world we know is possible because we're from there.

We are heirs to magic.
We are heirs to revolution.
We are heirs to dream.

Like a medieval tapestry, the works within tell a story, weaving in and out of each other with organic intent. Birthed in the dark half of the northern year, they speak of winter and death, of ending and carnival, of great manifestations of what we see best when there is little light. May the five chapters of this journal—adorned with the enchanting artwork and photography of Li Pallas, Aaron Shenewolf, Wespennest, and Lois Cordelia—remind you of everything we already are.

SINGING THE SONGS WE FORGOT

The first chapter is an incantation, a remembrance, a recollection of the melodies which create our world. Understanding how we became disenchanted, we may learn again to sing our world into being. Lia Hunter's piece, **The Enchanted**, breathes the air of hope back into lungs long-choked on despair. **Valdres Roots,** by James Lindenschmidt, tells the history of his ancestors and the echoing lament of their lost land. Poet and awenydd Lorna Smithers evokes for us the moment when the "Father of the Industrial Revolution"—Richard Arkwright—played the "**Devil's Bagpipes on**

Stoneygate." Another poet, Finnchuill, unravels the tangled knots of our disenchantment and displacement (and the men who got us there) in **Becoming Placed.**

THE WINTER OF OUR WORLD

In the Welsh Druidic tradition, the Midwinter Solstice is named Alban Arthan, "the light of the earth," and this chapter contemplates death and what is born from dark, frozen places. Druid Judith O'Grady opens with her contemplation of what will outlast the human in **Call To Cold Gods.** In **The Year Of Dark Epiphanies**, anarchist Margaret Killjoy recalls the search for God and the wisdom that comes from death. In carcass of Salmon and corpse of war-dead, Herbalist & witch Sean Donahue reminds us what cannot stay buried in **Restoring Life To Death.**

But what to do in a dying world? asks Pegi Eyers. Her answer, in **Contemplating the Ruins**, is to do what we've always done: tell stories. And in **Mysterium Tremendum**, poet and priest of Brigid Christopher Scott Thompson invokes our ancient inheritance from the frozen wastes.

THE MANIFESTATION OF THE UNSEEN

In magic and spirit-work, we speak of *manifestation*—making present our desires, embodying the Other. In Europe and elsewhere, a strike or protest is a manifestation, and in the spirit of throngs, rebels, and revelers gathered against the powerful, can we not see therin an in-dwelling? Is not, then, a manifesto itself a spell? In this chapter are seven works which explore what comes through our opened gates.

Druid & academic Jonathan Woolley follows the diverging transatlantic threads of Paganism in **The Matter of The Gods** to find, at their end, the weakening of Empire. In the "taming" of the old powers and thefts from goddesses in the Irish and Welsh Bardic tradition can be seen Man's arrogance over Nature; in **Response To Amergin**, poet Chris Worlow speaks the land's laughing reply. In **No Hope, No Despair,** anti-humanist Lo steals back the wisdom of Nihilism from the fatalists and offers it back to the gods. Writer and performer Heathen Chinese explores the question of a god's alliances in **Are The Gods On Our Side?** Poet, priest, and academic P. Sufenas Virius Lupus confronts the Anthropocene and the resurgence of goddess-worship in **Earth Goddesses Uprising.** Professor, animist, and ceremonial magician Kadmus unravels our modern conceptions of rights and proposes a radical—yet quite simple—framework for them in **Nature's Rights**. And academic and occultist Al Cummins leads us into the dark, desolate places in search of Saturnine revolt in **Dirt Sorcery**.

Joy Against the Machine

If rising seas, dying forests, authoritarian governments and wars for resources are all the death groans of Capital, then this chapter is our liberating laughter. In **Ned Ludd**, poet, academic, and author Yvonna Aburrow reminds us that, armed with hammers and the strength of the land, no machine can stand. Therapist, writer, and witch Anthony Rella gives voice to our symptoms in **The Soul Is A Site of Liberation.** In the leaps, gyres, and turns of the Witches Sabbat is an embodied truth that neither torture nor fire could still. Silvia Federici, author of *Caliban & The Witch*, celebrates the power of flesh with **In Praise Of The Dancing Body**. Mother, witch, and writer Niki Whiting reminds us that resistance can be bloody in **Our Bodies Are Not Machines**. Crippled by despair? In **Life Support Systems,** environmentalist and Lokean Fjothr Lokakvan will arm you with our greatest weapons: hope, joy, and love. And with arms outstreched in kindness, Reclaiming witch Mandrake calls you to **The Dare.**

The End & Everything After

The book which has most broken open the concrete in which the seeds of our beautiful resistance now grow is Peter Grey's *Apocalyptic Witchcraft*. Like the kind withered hands of Ceridwen, it beckoned us to see with unjudging eyes the end we all most fear—and smile.

The End & Everything After echoes this call—look upon the Apocalypse, embrace it, and see the deep roots of the worlds' forests nourished by Capital's ruin. Man's desolate dream to colonise other planets gets a sestina from dancer and poet Sajia Sultan in **Making Mars a Woman**. Max Oanad's short-story, **A Treatise On The Old Powers** is a warning from the future to those who would try to keep this system around. Priest, activist, and writer T. Thorn Coyle's poem, **The World Will End But We May Change** hears in the whistle of a kettle the sounds of Apocalypse. Virgilio Rivas turns the blade of critical theory upon our most central fear, revealing behind the question "how will we survive without all this?" and the false threat of the Katechon in **A Counter-Apocalypse For Out Time**. And regarding the 'end of civilisation,' druid Nimue Brown's poem **Natural Habitat** reminds us that the urban—civilization—is only where we choose to look, not where we ever really are. And finally, Rhyd Wildermuth tells a tale of winter against **Apparently Impossible Problems.**

May this journal remind you what you've always been, what you always shall be, what you always are. May these works awaken again your hope. May they remind you that you're not alone, struggling against an impossible system, an omnipotent Authority, an undying machine in the world's long winter. It is never long till the next spring.

May this journal be for you a hearth, a flame, a fire by which we can reforge our souls, a seed by which by which we may rewild the cities, a song by which we may Re-enchant the world.

> *In the difficulties of revolt, in the hardships of love,*
> *we become the struggle of seed through death-black soil*
> *reaching towards life in an unseen sun,*
> *reforging ever what shall become*
> *in the darkness of wet loam and dirt*
> *unfolding an entire world*
> *from everything we already are.*

Be well.
Dream well.
Resist Beautifully.

Rhyd Wildermuth
editor
bard of the Raven King, of the Hearthkeeper, of the Crown of the North, of the Bent White One, and of the Liberator

Seattle, Washington
15 October, 2015

Singing The Songs We Lost

IMBALANCE

Everything is spinning out of balance. The world is being polluted and corrupted, and it's decaying while still alive. Mega-storms, droughts, fracking quakes, and rising seas eat entire island nations and devastate helpless communities, which are then swarmed by hungry, opportunistic corporations that sell off and buy up what's left, and build hungry empire in their place. Entire mountains have been eaten by mining operations, which also leave the land and water around them toxified. Racism bides within social institutions and quietly mows down swaths of people of color, and stands on the necks of those who remain. Colonies of bees die off, Monarch butterflies cannot make their annual migration to overwinter and reproduce, hundreds of birds fall from the sky at once, mysteriously slain. Many, many species of Earthlings are going extinct and taking a lot of the balance and creative diversity of nature with them — taking pieces of the whole with them — now forever secret. Most members of our own species live difficult, oppressed lives in or under the purview of stratified societies and empires which invented poverty and wealth, race and class.

EMPIRES

What need did humanity have of empire, in its incredibly long existence? It had none, for hundreds of thousands of years —eons filled with kin and culture and integration with the abundant world. We had wholeness. Now we have fragmented, unbalanced lives being pushed by clocks, pulled by disjointed narratives and misconceptions, stomped by greed, and our only defense the solid reality of community, love, and nature--when we are lucky enough to find islands of it amidst the cacophony of ticking time-which-is-money, manufactured desires, and hyper-individualistic isolation in which this terminally ill culture is drowning. The decision to unbalance society and exclude all of the community (even the eco-community) except the men (and often only certain privileged men, at that) from the communal decision-making and interest-considering was one of the first steps on this unbalanced, destructive path.

The Enchanted
(Lia Hunter)

Pathological patriarchy arose to control women, and to ensure the tracking of sired children — tracking which hadn't been necessary in matrilineal societies that took care of all children. Some long-ago group of men thought they needed to ensure that their efforts would only benefit their own children, not the community. Selfishness triumphed over communal responsibility, and became codified into law.

Ownership and inheritance became important to them. Their society was stratifying, and they needed to get on top of the heap. The alternative was poverty and slavery. Dominance became important too. Having dominion over not only your family and community, but neighboring communities and even all living creatures became a cultural value and driving subtext in the script. If *empire*, then be *emperor*—or as close to it as you can get, otherwise you'll *be fodder*. A lot of fodder lies at the bottom, and only one emperor at the top, with an inverse pyramid of wealth held above and a heavy lack of enough resources below. Its pyramid shape of hierarchy is inherently unfair and unjust.

CULTURAL SCRIPT

We're still working from this script, a few thousand years later. But not for long. This script is not sustainable. This play chews up the set and buries most of its actors. There won't even be an audience left, at the end. This is not the only script ever performed, nor the only one possible. It's only the most recent. Imperialism is relatively new in human history. Capitalism is even newer – only about 300 years old — and even more destructive. Capitalism is a natural outgrowth of the kyriarchal complex of cultural concepts like patriarchy, dominionism, hegemony, colonialism, wealth, and hyper-individualism that have busily been infecting the cultures and peoples of Earth and rewriting their cultural DNA, re-scripting their histories and futures with lies and false promises.

And we can be done with it. We can cancel the terrible show and start writing and rehearsing, or even remembering one that does not eat our children and destroy mind, body, soul, Earth, and connection. It made us forget what community is, and what sacred means, but we can find them again. Some of us have already begun. Some of us in indigenous communities never lost them and can share them.

There are paths strewn with fulfillment rather than endless hunger. We can find the paths with vital air to breathe, clean water to refresh, and solid ground to stand and circle with each other upon. Our ancestors knew them, walked them, danced them. Some continued to remember them throughout empire, despite the illusions of usurious capital and divine right of kings, and preserved markers for us in myth, symbol, and language. Nature, itself, contains markers and inspiration. Our home and kin are calling us.

THE CALLING

We are some of the first in generations to hear the call of nature, spirits, gods, and ancestors, and our own connected souls. We are some of the first to gather again in circles and remember, to listen to wind and stars and to recall. We are organic circles of community, not mechanical pyramids of empire. We remember who we are, we remember all Earthlings are family, and we remember that we belong to the Earth — the Earth does not belong to us. We are now charged with finding the paths again and showing each other the way before this path leads an entire world into chaos and premature death. We must heal this sickness, for are we not the healers Earth has produced in her time of need? Do you not feel the calling of the oppressed, the ancestors, our children's children, and the Earth, *chanting* our names and the great need?

We are the enchanted, who will answer the call of justice and of healing, and re-enchant the world, singing up reconnection and dancing up a real future. We have the magic – will and intention, the calling and the help of truth. Let us be the good ancestors who take up these Witches' brooms, Druids' sickles, and Heathens' hammers to clear away, to build, and to relight the sacred flame at the heart of the world.

Lia Hunter

Lia Hunter is a poet and student of anthropology, environmental science, and Druidry. She has experienced 20+ years of life as a conservative Christian and, then nearly as many again as a progressive Pagan.
The experience of changing religions and rebuilding values made her an anthropologist, fascinated by culture and especially religion. It's easy enough from an anthropological perspective looking at social systems to see that capitalism is wildly destructive and that humanity needs sustainable systems, ASAP

Valdres Roots

(James Lindenschmidt)

Most people can find in their genealogy or in their own lives some point when their ancestors or they themselves were forced from lands and social relations that provided subsistence without having to sell either one's products or oneself, i.e., they suffered Enclosure. Without these moments of force, money would have remained a marginal aspect of human history. These moments were mostly of brutal violence, sometimes quick (with bombs, cannon, musket or whip), sometimes slower (with famine, deepening penury, plague), which led to the terrorized flight from the land, from the burnt-out village, from the street full of starving or plague-ridden bodies, to slave ships, to reservations, to factories, to plantations. This flight ended with "producers becoming more dependent on exchange" since they had no other way to survive but by either selling their products or selling themselves or being sold. Thus did "exchange become more independent of them," its transcendental power arising from the unreversed violence that drove "everyone" into the monetary system."

George Caffentzis, "The Power Of Money: Debt and Enclosure," In Letters Of Blood & Fire

*I*t is spring, 1870. My great-grandfather, Mons Olsen Fuglie, then an 8 1/2 year old boy, left his ancestral home in Valdres, Norway, traveling south to Kristiana (what had been, and is now, called Oslo). He boarded the Argonault under the command of Captain S.W. Flood, bound from Kristiana to land in Quebec, before continuing the journey to their new life in Minnesota. The journey across the Atlantic took two months, with 237 passengers aboard a ship whose length was 147.5 feet and beam 29 feet, depth of 11 feet. With Mons were his 3 siblings, his mother Ambjor Monsdatter and his father Ole Arneson. Pre-industrial transatlantic travel was grueling, so much so that Ole was weakened from the journey and collapsed, 25 days after landing in Minnesota, dying of what they called heat stroke. My great-grandfather thus grew up on a new continent, in a new ecosystem, in a place with new languages, without his father.

ANCESTRAL HOMELANDS?

I don't remember hearing much about displacement when I was growing up in a mid-western middle class suburbia in the 70s and 80s. When I did, it was usually the standardized, whitewashed account of slavery in the Americas, where African people were kidnapped from their homelands, taken against their will in slave ships across the Atlantic, and inserted into the capitalist system as slaves. In one sense, I was lucky that my high school had a good racial mixture of people. European-Americans like myself were the majority, but there were a lot of African-Americans and Asian-Americans as well. Despite an interest in my genealogy as a child, I never thought much about displacement as it applies to my own life and ancestry until the past decade or two. It is no accident that I have also spent this time cultivating my connection with place, as part of my spiritual practice.

It is also no accident that this spiritual connection with place was developed around the same time I moved to Maine. Maine is an extraordinary place, with astounding ecosystems and nature spirits. I have an ocean, beaches (both sandy and rocky), marshlands, mountains, rivers, forests, springs, small cities, lakes, ponds, parks, trails, and farms all within an hour's drive of my home. I have spent more time in nature in the 1/3 of my life in Maine than all the other places I have lived or visited. I have slowly picked up a rudimentary knowledge of the ecosystem, learning to identify plants, trees, animal tracks, scat, game trails, and geological formations. I find it fascinating, but despite all I've learned, I know that my knowledge is dwarfed by the knowledge any child who has seen 8 summers in an indigenous culture with an ancestral connection to place would have. Despite my increasing comfort level with the ecosystem here in Maine, I know and recognize that I am "from away" (in the local parlance).

As beautiful as Maine is, and as much as I love "my" 2 acres of it, I know that on some level — the most primal, ancestral level — that I don't really belong here. I have no doubt that the Arossagunticook people who lived here for hundreds of generations prior to the arrival of the Europeans would concur.

Maine is also as close as I can get to my ancestral homelands without leaving the US. I'm sure the fact that I ended up here is a coincidence. *Of course.*

VALDRES ROOTS & HUSFOLK

"The visitor to Valdres ... by traversing its whole length between Spirilen and the wilds where Sogn meets Gudbrandsdalen, with excursions into the many spots of beauty or grandeur on either side... has the opportunity of seeing some of the best that is to be found of practically all elements of scenic attractions that Norway offers the sightseer anywhere, and he will understand why the native of Valdres thinks his Valley the most beautiful region of all the old Fatherland.'"

For dozens of generations, my Norwegian ancestors were *Husfolk* — "land tenants" who subsisted in mostly feudal ar-

---

1   Andrew A. Veblen, *Book of Valdris*, p 19

As a result of the lack of "opportunity" in Norway, 900,000 Norwegians emigrated to America between 1825-1914, such that by 1920, there were more people in America descendant from Valdres than there were people left in Valdres.

rangements with the landed lords — in Valdres, a *fogderi* (county) in southern, central Norway, just south of the Jotunheimen mountains. From 1750-1850, the population of Norway doubled, from about 700,000 to 1.4 million. This was the period of Enclosure in Norway, which drove my ancestors from their subsistence on the land, and destroyed the ancestral link they had with it. Much of the potential farmland—that had lain uncultivated and intact since the Black Plague in the 1300s—was enclosed as private property. For the *Husfolk*, this gave them fewer options; since they didn't own land and had no way to buy it, they could only be subsumed within the labor exploitation of capitalism. Yet, industry hadn't really come to Norway, certainly not to the Valdres valley away from the cities. As a result of the lack of "opportunity" in Norway, 900,000 Norwegians emigrated to America between 1825-1914, such that by 1920, there were more people in America descendant from Valdres than there were people left in Valdres.

One can see the appeal for the landless Norwegians to emigrate to America, particularly in post-slavery America, the land of "manifest destiny," provided they were courageous (or desperate) enough to risk the frontier, with its wildness and the remaining packets of resistance from the Indigenous peoples protecting their ancestral claims to the land.

My ancestors, therefore, left Norway for both sides of the capitalist Enclosure coin. Norway had been completely enclosed, and too many people were there without land rights struggling to eke out a living. On the other hand, in the so-called New World (or if you prefer, Turtle Island), Enclosure hadn't yet fully begun. If you went far enough west., there remained millions of acres of fertile land and far fewer Europeans to claim them. So while my ancestors were being pushed out of Norway, they were also being pulled toward Minnesota.

BLOOD ROOTS & MUD ROOTS

"The ancestors are such an important part of our spiritual tradition. When we call to our ancestors in ritual and prayers, we may be asking for specific guidance from those who are conscious of our existence and coherent in their form, but perhaps more poignantly we are waking our own perception to their unceasing presence. We speak of their stories humming in our blood and bones, and this is true in terms of our genetic inheritance, yet felt too in the sense of their presence being *everywhere*. We speak of the breath we breathe having been breathed by our ancestors, and in this too we accept the practical logic of our globe's one body of air, yet also in the poetry and omnipresence of their consciousness.[2]"

I never knew my grandfather, Milton. Cancer claimed him long before I was born, when my mother was 12. Mons, Milton's father, also died when Milton was a child, having been kicked by a horse. So along with Ole, who died shortly after arriving in Minnesota, the three consecutive generations preceding me all grew up without their paternal connection to their homeland. This is, through my mother, grandfather, and great-grandfather, my connection to Valdres. I find it interesting that despite these generations of disconnect, I feel the strongest connection to this quarter of my family tree, over and above my Irish (Mom's Mom's side) and German (Dad's side) ancestry.

In Druidry, we talk about Mud Roots and Blood Roots. Mud Roots are a connection to a particular place. Blood Roots are those who came before—the ancestors. For more than a thousand years, as far back past history and into mythology as we can see, until the late 19th century, these Blood and Mud Roots were intertwined in Valdres, until the connection was broken by the capitalist enclosure movement.

This ancestral connection to place was strong enough to withstand centuries of hardship, famine, plague, warfare, the imposition of Christianity by force (spearheaded by Olaf the Saint, another one of my ancestors, but that's another story), not to mention a thousand harsh Norwegian winters, only to finally be destroyed by something so powerful, yet so insidious, that people today have to be taught what "enclosure" means. The notion of "private property" remains so abstracted, such a given, that many believe it has always existed. They assume that feudal Lords "owned" property in the same way as today's landlords, that serfs were much

The notion of "private property" remains so abstracted, such a given, that many believe it has always existed

closer to slave status than we ever could be in these enlightened times. On the contrary, as Silvia Federici reminds us:

The most important aspect of serfdom, from the viewpoint of the changes it introduced in the master-servant relation, is that it gave the serfs direct access to the means of their reproduction. In exchange for the work which they were bound to do on the lords' land (the *demesne*), the serfs received a plot of land (*mansus* or *hide*) which they could use to support themselves, and pass down to their children.... Having the effective use and possession of a plot of land meant that the serfs could always support themselves and, even at the peak of their confrontations with the lords, they could not easily be forced to bend because of the fear of starvation. True, the lord could throw recalcitrant serfs off the land, but this was rarely done, given the difficulty of recruiting new laborers in a fairly closed economy and the collective nature of peasant struggles.[3]"

The *Husfolk* of Valdres, therefore, were not slaves, or mere servants of the lordly class in Norway. There was a powerful bond between them and their place, a bond that, by the mid-1800s, after more than a century of capitalism and Enclosure, had grown weak enough that more than half the population of Norway had been displaced.

It is only in the past 300 years — far less than 1% of *homo sapiens* time on this planet — that we must distinguish between mud roots and blood roots. Prior to that, as rates of migration were much slower, they were much more intimately intertwined.

DOMESTICATION & THE CAPITALIST ACCUMULATION OF LABOR

"In the aftermath of the Black Death, every European country began to condemn idleness, and to persecute vagabondage, begging, and refusal of work. England took the initiative with the Statute of 1349 that condemned high wages and idleness (author's note: with higher wages, workers could work fewer hours and therefore had more leisure time), establishing that those who did not work, and did not have any means of survival, had to accept work. Similar ordinances were issued in France in 1351, when it was recommended that people should not give food or hostel to healthy beggars and vagabonds. A further ordinance in 1354 established that those who remained idle, passing their time in taverns, playing dice or begging, had to accept work or face the consequences; first offenders would be put in prison on bread and water, while second offenders would be put in the stocks, and third offenders would be branded on the forehead."[4]

After my great-grandfather Mons settled in Minnesota, where he lived until he died in 1925, he raised a large family there. But displacement caused by capitalism would strike again, this time in the form of the Great Depression. It would cause my grandfather to leave most of his family in Minnesota and settle in Ohio with his

---

2   Emma Restall-Orr, *Living Druidry*, p 204-5.

3   Silvia Federici, *Caliban & The Witch*, 23-4
4   Federici, 57-8.

sister and her husband. In due course, he met my grandmother, married, and started a family before his premature death in 1958.

So of course, **the winners of this game—severing of ancestral connections to place—are, and continue to be, the capitalists.** A people united with the land they occupy will give much more formidable resistance to Enclosure, accumulation of land and labor, and exploitation of all the resources it can. A divided, domesticated people severed from their ancestral place can offer no such resistance. Capitalism requires workers to exploit, and most people, given the choice, will not enter into such an exploitative relationship. Therefore, the choice had to go, and capitalism had to make people more dependent on what they were offering. Human domestication, via displacement and other strategies, had to be stepped up to a new level.

By most estimates, human domestication has been underway for 10,000 years, but it has accelerated dramatically in the capitalist era. Ostensibly, it doesn't matter where we live now. Just in my generation of my family, a few stayed in Ohio (where they'd been for only 2 generations), but I have siblings or cousins in Indiana, California, Kentucky, Minnesota, and Missouri. As strangers in strange lands, our domestication and dependence on the infrastructures of industrialized production grows more complete and absolute – not only are we uprooted from our ancestral homelands, but our connection with any place at all is broken. How many of us have a sense of place where we humans are part of an ecosystem, when the majority of us go not to the land for subsistence, but to the grocery store, buying factory-farmed food that has traveled thousands of miles before landing on the shelves?

Domestication is what happens when a connection to land is severed, and subsistence, provided by an industrial infrastructure, becomes abstracted from place. At one time, exile was a fate as bad as, or worse than, death: it meant one had little or no access to subsistence via the tribe, a collection of people working together for the common good. In this new, domesticated world, access to the tribe is mediated by money. Those without money — the poor among us — become exiles who must fend for themselves. And the quickest way to end one's exile is to allow oneself to be (re-)assimilated into the capitalist system of labor exploitation.

> *Capitalism requires workers to exploit, and most people, given the choice, will not enter into such an exploitative relationship.*

LOOKING AHEAD

My daughter, unlike I who am still "from away," is a Mainer. She was born in Portland and has never lived more than 20 miles from the city of her birth. She still most strongly resonates with the streets of Portland, rather than the far more rural area where we live now. I wonder, having grown up in this place, how her children and subsequent generations will be connected to their places, and whether their place will be in Maine.

The world is undone. In the age of neoliberal capitalism, otherwise known as "globalization," our people and our cultures are scattered to the four winds. Most ancestries in the 21st century are intertwined and complex; the stories I have told of my ancestors above are but one branch of my genealogy. Virtually everyone is, in some way, a victim of ancestral displacement, and my point is not to level out the differences between the different cultural victims of displacement, colonialism, and capitalist enclosure. While nearly all people of nearly all cultures, races, ethnicities, and groups have now experienced displacement, the fact is that my ancestors who arrived in Minnesota found themselves inserted into a different place in the power hierarchy than earlier peoples from Africa, kidnapped from their ancestral homeland, to be slaves in the Americas.

Re-enchanting the world will not occur in an office, in the checkout queue at Whole Foods, or in the blogosphere. It will require humans to get out into nature, and work ceaselessly to re-establish relationship with what they find there. There are some positives we can take from this situation we find ourselves in — for instance, most geneticists agree that diversity in our gene pools is a good thing — but until we exist in better relationship with our place, rewild ourselves, resist our domestication by rejecting the infrastructures of capitalism where we can, and begin re-weaving an ancestral connection to place for future generations, the world will remain little more than something to be owned and exploited. •

James Lindenschmidt

Moving between Animist & Panentheist, Druid & Heathen, Bard & Philosopher, Anarchist & Autonomist, feeding his spirit by bonding with his ecosystem, and learning to work with it in better and better relationship. He views fermentation as a devotional practice, with mead being the highest alchemical expression of an ecosystem.

Devil's Bagpipes on Stoneygate
(Lorna Smithers)

When Richard Arkwright played the devil's bagpipes on Stoneygate a giant hush came over the town. The blistering whirring sound against the pink horizon of a sun that would not set over clear sights for two centuries of soot and smog was damnable. Yes damnable! Gathering in storm clouds over Snape Fell.

You who have seen a premonition might have heard the village seers tell of smoke for flesh charry knees and the squalor of shanty towns. Red brick mills turning satanic faces to the coin of their heliotropic sun: Empire.

Piecers running between generations bent legged beggers, tongue in cheek defiant. Weavers watching shuttles slipping through fingers like untamed flies. Luddites sweeping across greens with armaments and gritted teeth. The new need-fires of burnt-out mills. Staggerings of Chorley.

How he rubbed gristly chubby jaws and did not see the unfairness of profit or tightly curled hair when hair-pin thin people laboured in his thrall. How he played the devil's bagpipes over breached bones of the dead then one day toppled pot-bellied splay-legged from his cushy stool.

In bugle layers of this town decided long ago I long to rush through industrial rain, knock and knock on his front door and beg him to stop. But know he will not listen. Only play on and on laughing his demonic laugh. So we dance the hurly-burly on the ruins of Horrocks' back yard in a splash of flowers and cement as if it is our last.

Lorna Smithers

lives in Penwortham, Lancashire. She writes poems for unsung landscapes and myths for unacknowledged gods. In January 2015 she published her first collection of poetry and stories Enchanting the Shadowlands. You can find her performing in cafes and libraries, enchanted woodlands and on mist-wrapped hills and blogging at 'From Peneverdant' https://lornasmithers.wordpress.com

The word enchantment literally means using chant/song to lay a spell, coming to English by way of French from the Late Latin, incanttorem; Latin to sing: cantare (Oxford Dictionary of English Etymology). Related to incantation. All derived from kan-, a reconstructed Indo-European root for song [5].

THE MAGIC GARDEN

Max Weber wrote that pre-industrial western Europe, before the rise of capitalist relations, was a magic garden. By that, he meant most people experienced the natural world as full of fairies, goblins, sprites and a nearly endless variety of spirits; the domestic realm, likewise, had its spirits. And the dead were thought to return from time to time.

The universal doctrines of Christianity had only partially rolled back the animist world of pagan times, and the Catholic world itself was one of angels, demons who wandered in inhabited places, and the magical powers and interventions of saints and their relics. The efforts of the clergy had been unable to stop beliefs in phenomena such as the Wild Hunt, the Good Game of Diana, the practices of the Friulian benandanti (the good walkers)[6], fairy doctoring, and many others among peasant populations even by the 1500s (and later). Miners propitiated spirits and believed veins of metal grew in underground trees, and during the Renaissance, among educated classes, alchemists and magicians worked with spirits in their practices and had philosophies that, while slotted into Christian overarching beliefs, were far from orthodox.

The doctor, medical alchemist, botanist, toxicologist, and subversive Paracelsus is a revealing example. Born in Switzerland in 1493, educated at the Universities of Basel and Ferrara, he led a life of wandering, and provoked the authorities in various cities as he helped the poor for free. He emphasized both observation and what we would call magical methods, like the use of talismans and astrology for cures. He learned from the common people, especially from miners, barbers, bathkeepers, and women healers.

Becoming Placed (Finnchuill)

---

5   (Watkins)
6   See the works of Carlo Ginzburg, a brilliant Italian historian, such as *The Night Battles*.

His work *The Philosophy Addressed to the Athenians* provides a glimpse of this current of Renaissance thought and of its enchanted world. Here he puts forth a vitalist philosophy of nature as a *mysterium magnum*, a mother that generates the four elements—active living forces that unfold through various objects over time. Each element was a mother of a world, including living creatures, minerals, and spirits—worlds full of creatures irrational and rational. From water come nymphs, sirens, drams, lorinds, nesder, marine monsters, as well as lakes, springs, rivers, seas, certain stones, fleshy animals, and marine plants. From the earth come forth: gnomes, sylvesters, lemurs, giants, as well as minerals, gems, stones, fruits, flowers, and seeds. From the air: witches, and sylphs; from fire: salamanders, stars, the sun and other celestial objects, plus certain minerals and flowers. It was a conception of reality where humans were but one of the many tribes of nature, and not the noblest. Magic was nearly ubiquitous at the time, every village having a 'wizard' or wise person who used spells, chants, talismans for healing, finding lost objects and the like. Magic was done through aid, alliance, and manipulation of other spirit persons, not by vague energies or physical forces.

Bacon strongly influenced the development of the ideology of modern science, and his rhetoric is especially revealing in his disdain for the natural world and how it must be violently interrogated.

DISENCHANTMENT AND HOW WE BECAME UNPLACED

One key player in the western history of disenchantment, Francis Bacon (1561-1626), had an enormous impact on the development of science, particularly in shifting from a vitalist, animist view of world to a mechanistic worldview of dead matter. This included a momentous shift from seeing nature as a nurturing motherly figure (who had a fierce side, too) to a disordered but largely passive female figure to be held down, exploited, and essentially stripped of agency.

To understand Bacon and his thinking, it's necessary to understand his historical context of religious struggles, his Puritan sympathies, a backdrop of increasing value placed on technical skills, poor-laws, collapses of guilds, and enclosures. His father had benefited from the great upheavals caused by the closing of the monasteries and the seizing and redistribution of the vast lands of the Catholic Church under the Protestant English monarchs. This was also a time of enclosures of common lands and popular resistance against this. As the subsistence economy of feudal times was increasingly disrupted and broken up, large numbers of displaced people were on the roads—vagabonds and migrant laborers. In rural England the cloth industry as well as mining became important sites for a shift from craft to pre-industrial capitalism. This is the world Bacon grew up in, amidst what Max Weber called the rise of the Protestant ethic and the spirit of capitalism. By the late 1500s, the position of women had decreased, as well.

Bacon was in government and flourished under James I (James VI of Scotland), who in his younger years was paranoid of being harmed by witches (and even thought he had almost been drowned by their spells during a voyage with his bride from Norway to Britain). The king wrote a famous tract on diabolical witchcraft, the *Daemonomologie* (1597). He also enacted harsher laws against witchcraft in 1603; under Elizabeth I the death penalty was reserved only for those who had murdered by witchcraft, but now the king's law made a capital offense of any use of witchcraft.[7]

Bacon was very aware of the investigations and procedures that were used at the time on the bodies of women in witchcraft investigations, and that rhetoric would permeate his scientific work. He had participated as attorney general (appointed in 1613) in the Sir Thomas Overbury murder case. He brought charges against the Countess of Somerset, Frances Howard, who—angered by a poem published by Overbury that opposed her romance with the man to become her husband, Robert Carr—with an accomplice, a woman named Mrs. Turner, poisoned Overbury. The countess confessed but was spared execution, though Mrs. Turner was not. It was a case that got lots of publicity, with much ink spilt about disorderly women assuming masculine roles and fashions. The countess wore ruffs, which were considered by men a masculine prerogative. Bacon would also have been aware of the trials of the Pendle Forest witches in 1612, where the Continental charge of sex with the devil first appeared in England, as well as other witch trials and their use of torture in investigations.

Bacon strongly influenced the development of the ideology of modern science, and his rhetoric is especially revealing in

---

7   (Merchant 168)

his disdain for the natural world and how it must be violently interrogated. Nature continued to be viewed as a female, but in Bacon's thought no longer as a mother—instead, she was a disordered female in need of domination and even torture. He also saw himself very much at odds with the Renaissance magus and with the alchemist. The Renaissance magician aimed to assist nature, but Bacon thought nature needed to be 'vexed' to yield her secrets for man[8]:

> "The magus was wrong in thinking his effort was to assist nature."[9]

He proposed a new operating procedure:

> "For you have but to follow and as it were hound nature in her wanderings, and you will be able when you like to lead and drive her afterward to the same place again.....Neither ought a man to make scruple of entering and penetrating these holes and corners, when the inquisition of truth is his whole object—as your majesty has shown in your own example," (referencing King James, his patron)[10]

Scientific knowing required forcing of its object:

> "For like as a man's disposition is never well known or proved till he be crossed, nor Proteus ever changed shapes till he was straitened and held fast, so nature exhibits herself more clearly under the trials and vexations of art (mechanical devices) than when left to herself."[11]

His rhetoric of the womb is particularly revealing:

> "There is therefore much ground for hoping that there are still laid up in the womb of nature many secrets of excellent use having no affinity or parallelism with anything that is now known...only by the method which we are not treating can they be speedily and suddenly and simultaneously presented and anticipated."

A huge amount of texts and visual art portrayed women as not only inferior but as closer to nature, and a nature more and more portrayed as wild and disorderly. The new discourse firmly placed culture and the new science as the opposite side of nature. Contradictorily, women were said to be challenging their place in nature. Protestant preachers like John Knox had been horrified at the event of queens, as can be seen in his tract, *The Blast of the Trumpet Against The Monstrous Regiment of Women* (1558). Unsurprisingly, the status of actual women was declining as the capitalist economy became more dominant, a few queens excepted.

Nature being female for Bacon warranted new methods of inquiry:

> "She is either free and follows her ordinary course of development as in the heaven, in the animal and vegetable creation, and in the general array of the universe; or she is driven out of her ordinary course by the perverseness, insolence, and forcedness of matter and violence of impediments, as in the case of monsters; or lastly, she is put in constraint, modeled, and made as it were new by art and the hand of man; as in things artificial"[12]

Nature would not come on her own—she had to be bound and forced. Bacon thought miners and smiths had been the pioneers. People should forsake *"Minerva and the Muses as barren virgins, to rely upon Vulcan."*[13] Alchemists should throw out their books. Go completely empirical and materialist, in other words.

Bacon believed man could recover the power over nature that had been lost when Adam and Eve were cast out of the Garden of Eden. According to historian Carolyn Merchant, a key strategy for Bacon in his posthumously published *The New Atlantis* was overturning strictures against manipulative magic that had been prevalent in the 16th century, as in Agrippa's 1530 publication, *Vanity of Arts and Science*.[14] The new system of investigation-- that is, modern science-- would combine mechanical technology and the new empirical method of science, a "New Organon"[3]. It aimed *"to endeavor to establish and extend the power and dominion of the human race itself over the universe"*. Bacon believed this was a divine bequest to man[15].

And so a new objectivity was made: the role of observing. As Ran Priur, a green anarchist, has written: *"To observe*

Bacon believed man could recover the power over nature that had been lost when Adam and Eve were cast out of the Garden of Eden

---

8   This was a challenge to the conventional Aristotelianism of the medieval scholastics, who revered Aristotle's *Organon*.

9   (Merchant, 171)

10   (Merchant, 168)

11   (Merchant, 171)

12   (Merchant, 170).

13   (Merchant, 171)

14   (Merchant, 184)

15.   This is most decidedly gendered for Bacon.

something is to perceive it while distancing oneself emotionally and physically, to have a one-way channel of "information" moving from the observed thing to "self", which is defined as not being part of that things."[16]

THE NEW ATLANTIS

Bacon's most ambitious book was *The New Atlantis*, published in 1627, a year after his death. Here he envisions a utopia with research facilities that eerily foreshadow contemporary laboratories. A highly scientific and Christian (Protestant, of course) culture is revealed in the remoteness of the southern reaches of the Pacific, a small continent named Bensalem. It is governed by a patriarchal scientific body named Salomon's House.

The narrator of this fiction was on a ship that had been sailing from Peru to Asia but became adrift in the infamous doldrums—and for such a long time

that its stocks ran perilously low. But at the time of their direst need they saw clouds piling up on the horizon, a sign of land. Soon it turns out that they have been sighted, a small boat comes up to theirs and escorts them into the harbor of this land. There they are quarantined. The oddest thing about this scientific nation is that they are unknown to Europe, Asia, and the rest of the world but they know about every nation, having been surveilling them for centuries. They are aware of current events as well as the history of the nations.

Salomon's House practitioners seem almost omniscient, casting their scientific gaze across the planet. Its agents have long disguised themselves as members of various cultures, passing among them incognito, then returning with their reports and surveys. The governor who visits the sequestered men from the ship questions their selected elite and answers some questions, and reveals the history of his hidden nation.

Long ago their nation had been better known; he reveals the tale of how Bensalem had converted to Christianity via the descent of a mysterious pillar of light which rotated on the nearby sea, and which revealed a box containing the

Bible. In the ensuing years a blend of science and religion had proliferated; the eye of Bensalem, as the country was called, seems like a colossal and haunting eye that is able to veil itself (some mythic resonance there). A vision of science invisible, yet always gazing on a world that it has penetrated, is a trope that would play out tremendously in centuries to come.

Nineteen hundred years previously, this Atlantis of the Pacific was governed by a Platonic philosopher-king named Salomon who founded the Institute, called both Salomon's House and the College of the Six Days' Works. The governor related to the men that the House was named for the Hebrew king and that it held the book of Natural History written by that wise king—a work that had been lost to the rest of the world. Through familiarity with this text and cataloguing of the Biblical God's works had come the other name of the College. This shows the heart of Bacon's ideology: namely that the earth had been created for man, and that it was time that men learned how to use all of the resources that the Christian God had provided, which lay in wait. In utilitarian fashion all species and aspects of the planet inherently existed for human exploitation, and with the incipient scientific method they were ripe for the taking.

"The end of our foundation is the knowledge of causes, and secret motions of things, and the enlarging of the bounds of human empire, to the effecting of all things possible".[17]

The governor goes on to describe Salomon's House and some of its key projects: it is an amazing document with Bacon being quite prescient about many things to come. There are deep underground mines and chambers where various experiments are carried out as well as high towers up to half a mile in height with observatories. There are establishments which sound remarkably like places for genetic engineering:

> "We have means to make...diverse new plants, differing from the vulgar. By art likewise, we make them greater or taller than their kind is, and contrariwise barren and not generative; also we make them different in color, shape, activity— many new kinds....We make a number of serpents, worms, flies, fishes, of putrefaction, whereas some are advanced (in effect) to be perfect creatures, like beasts or birds, and have sexes, and do propagate. Neither do we do this by chance, but we know beforehand, of what matter and commixture, what kind of those creatures will arise."[18]

Sounds like a manifesto for Monsanto. Bensalem's shadow could be the plastic continent now arising in the eastern Pacific, the so-called Great Garbage Patch between Hawaii and California.

From such visions the laboratory science of Robert Boyle (1627-1691) would be grounded later in the century (which has set the tone for lab science to the present). Boyle emphasized the need to not just know nature but to dominate her. A great admirer of Bacon, he saw even more than the 'master' the important connections between the new method, the mechanistic view, and commercial middle class interests.[19] This new science would be stamped with a Protestant character: sober and chaste as technoscience remains.

Science historian and theorist Donna Haraway writes of the knowledge produced, which was:

> "constructed to have the ground-breaking capacity to ground social order objectively, literally. This separation of expert knowledge from mere opinion as the legitimating

One of the fronts for the practical application of the new mechanistic ideology was the new capitalist agriculture, which claimed all lands could be 'improved' upon.

knowledge for ways of life, without appeals to transcendent authority or to abstract uncertainty of any kind, is a founding gesture of what we call modernity."[20]

Immeasurable violence was required for its founding.

One of the fronts for the practical application of the new mechanistic ideology was the new capitalist agriculture, which claimed all lands could be 'improved' upon. Land would be improved for increased yields and would augment the status of this new type of farmer. In England it also involved displacing people already on the land for the making of short term profits. Various how-to handbooks were published, including *The English Improver Improved*, by William Blith (1652). Draining fens and bogs are mentioned on its title page[21]. One of the regions targeted by 17th century enclosure and 'improving' was the fen country north of London and Cambridge, which had been a network of marshes and meres, much of it flooded in winter, the margins of which provided pasturage in the summer and supported vast numbers of birds and other wetlands life.

The Dutch had pioneered drainage techniques, but mostly for reclaiming land from the sea. Dutch capitalists financed drainage of marshes in other European countries. There was much resistance to the enclosures, the draining of wetlands and loss of common lands, and the deprival of rights to use woods for sustenance. The fen dwellers took to destroying sluices, knocking down fences, and destroying the newly planted grain of the enclosures. The fen dwellers' inspiring tavern protest songs reveal a life lived in deep relationality, and of their heart-breaking loss as early agribusiness interests drained the fens. Here is a fen song from the 1630's:

> Come brethren of the water, let us all assemble,
> To treat upon this matter, which makes us quake and tremble
> For we shall rue it, if't be true, that Fens be undertaken,
> And where we feed in fen and reed, they'll feed both Beef and Bacon.
> The feathered Fowls have wings to fly to other nations;
> but we have no such things, to help our transportations;
> We must give place (oh grievous case) to horned beast and cattle
> Except that we canal agree to drive them out by battle[22].

---

17 (Bacon, 312)
18 (Bacon, 324)
19 (Merchant 187)

20 (Haraway, 24))
21 (Merchant, 55)
22 (Merchant, 60)

Newton and Descartes on Space

Disenchantment led to the dissolution of place into space, conceptually, a key component of place's erasure. Rene Descartes was the other foundation stone for the mechanistic view of the world; this French philosopher was so different from Bacon in his emphasis on rationalism rather than empiricism, but their philosophies would come together in the defining scientific method. For Descartes, science was a "universal mathematics.[23]" Space and matter were extension. Nature was geometry, via its essential shapes everything material could be understood, at least if broken down to simple components; then it could be put back together. So Descartes was most interested in measurability. For him, place was a subordinate feature of matter and space, parasitic on *res extensa*. Mind (*res cogitans*) was completely split off from matter, subject and object fully severed.

Isaac Newton found Descartes' facts generally wrong but his principles essential; that nature was an immense machine, atomistic and mechanical, obeying mathematical rules (Berman 30). Like Galileo he combined rationalism and empiricism, but his zeitgeist was ripe for this view (unlike Galileo, who had lived his last years under house arrest), and Newton stamped science with his imprint—positivity, atomism, and experimental method became "reality."

For Newton, place becomes nothing but a placeholder of measurement. Place is dissolved into absolute space, place at best becomes a marker. Places are conceived as mere parts of space; the geometrizing of space that occurs there belongs properly to mechanics, that is to laws governing material bodies at rest, or in motion....the aim of Newtonian geometry is measurement.

> "*Therefore, geometry is founded in mechanical practice,*' says Newton, and is "*nothing but the part of universal mechanics which accurately proposes and demonstrates the art of measuring.*" But the basis of measuring in precisely the regularity, the homogeneity of the space to be measured. In this way, too, the triumph of space over place is assured, given that implacement, moving into place asks merely to be experienced or perceived, not to be measured...*"[24]

This radical predominance of Space (and its corollary of measurability) occurs within the *Weltanschauung* of the early capitalism of the times. It can hardly be accidental that as a new economic orientation, capitalism, for which everything was resource to be used, measured, sold for profit, that the absolutism of space-- which dissolved all places-- reigned. A dissolution happening while place after place was being conquered, and peoples decimated and enslaved in vast new worlds, whose wealth needed to be measured and sent to the elites of western Europe. It can hardly be accidental that as a new economic orientation, capitalism, for which everything was resource to be used, measured, sold for profit, that the absolutism of space—which dissolved all places—reigned.

According to Jesus Sepulveda, "*...the West marched along imposing the scientific instrumental rationality that justifies colonial practices and universal models.*"[25]

The construction of race was part of this: "*This notion is the direct consequence of technological thinking that categorizes human experience and standardizes reality*"[26].

Even the illimitable regions of the sea were lined with longitude and latitude. **All must be measured, quantified and made open, after being stripped of qualities.** Everything could be standardized. Truth was utility. Facts stripped of values, enabling standardization wielded by instrumental reason. 'Progress'. All the tools for Disenchantment, *Entzauberung der Welt*, Max Weber's term for this watershed event, assembled and wielded.

Philosopher Edward Casey quotes Cisco Lassiter on the interchangeability that has become ubiquitous in modern life:

> "*for the modern self, all places are essentially the same: in the uniform, homogenous space of the Euclidean-Newtonian grid, all places are essentially interchangeable. Our homes, even our places for homes are defined by objective measures*" (Getting Back).

It can hardly be accidental that as a new economic orientation, capitalism, for which everything was resource to be used, measured, sold for profit, that the absolutism of space—which dissolved all places—reigned.

---

23 (Berman 20)

24 (Casey 147)

25 (Sepulveda, 29)

26 (Sepulveda, 29)

People now spend so much time in *sites*, as opposed to *places*, including malls and shopping centers, office buildings, and transportation corridors. Airports are a paragon of these de-placed spaces; and flying is the quintessential modern activity. In consideration of all this I keep wondering why do Pagans always talk about **space**, creating sacred space and so on, but not much about **place**?

THE POWER OF THE IMAGINATION/REENCHANTMENT

"To uncover the hidden history of place is to find a way back into the place world—a way to savor the renascence of place even on the most recalcitrant terrain." Edward Casey.

Listening to the land, to the particularities of a place can feel like finding water in the desert of space. We may live in displaced environments, but by listening attentively, becoming enchanted again, we can learn to pay heed to our places. Gathering everything that we can, scraps of history, science-based knowledge, community stories, tales, personal gnosis....

Consider, first, a return to place from the modern deserts of space by way of body, as the body was one way a preliminary sense of place returned to western philosophy; it is hard—if even possible at all—to be implaced if not embodied[27]. Phenomenologist philosopher, Maurice Merleau-Ponty wrote, *"The body is our general medium for having a world.*[28]*"*

For him, the orientation of the body and expressive movement gave *inhabitation*. The lived body is "anchorage in the world", not in homogenous space, but in familiar settings.

For a lived body, place is both a material experience and a transcendent expressive one,[29] which leads to a consideration of the expressive quality of poetic language and of myth as ways of knowing and therefore a key component in our reenchantment.

There are many ways to come back to place, but to return to a *sacred* sense of place, most important is reviving the mythic imagination. Talcott Parsons in his English translation of Max Weber's writing wrote that the western mind

Listening to the land, to the particularities of a place, can feel like finding water in the desert of space.

had been put into an 'iron cage' in its disenchantment, a cage of instrumental control. A more literal translation is that people had been encased in a shell as hard as steel[30]. This powerfully gets at what the disenchanted mind is, and in its dissolution is the reenchantment of the world.

Obviously, such encasement didn't work for everybody, people in peripheral areas, people labeled mad, or others working in various counter-traditions. But the institutions of the west are built of disenchantment, discourses zealously guard it, and often relegate peoples who are not western as inferior because their lives may still be enchanted; our children are schooled/disciplined into it.

We are taught as we grow older that fairy tales, myths and the like are pleasant pastimes for small children, but we should cast off such thinking, along with invisible friends, taking dreams seriously, and the like. If we dissolve the steel-like casing, there is much that can be hard to communicate in a society that only accepts the measureable and the literally empirical.

A consideration of the history of mythos and logos can help ground our practices of reenchantment. The roots of the displacement of mythic thought in the mainstream of western civilization go much further back than the early modern era I've been discussing, and take us back to classical Greece. Archaic and Homeric Greeks lived in a world of enchantment worded by their poets. Ancient poets actually met the Muses: like Hesiod, as he had on a mountain when he was a shepherd; the meeting utterly transformed his life. Archilocus had a similar experience: taking his father's cow to market he met the Muses on the road; they took the cow and left him a lyre in exchange. Sappho practiced in the context of intimate Aphrodite worship. Poets of the Homeric era (see the portrayal and performance of Demodocus in the Odyssey) and the archaic age performed truth for their societies, just as later vision poets (the *filid*, *awenyddion*, and *bardds*) did in Celtic cultures, and many others. But with the great changes exemplified by the rise of urban classical Athens, poetry as a way of knowing was challenged.

With the development of an urban, commercial society, an orientation to the written word—specifically the development of prose—occurred in a proliferation of legal and prag-

---

27 Non-corporal bodies still reference those of the sense world.
28 (Casey, Fate of Place, 233)
29 (Casey, Getting Back Into Place, 38)

30 The original German is *stahlhartes Gehäuse*: shell as hard as steel.

matic texts. While surprising reversals between the meaning of the terms *logos* and *mythos* occurred more than once, in terms of the definition deeply embedded in English usage (*false stories*) it was the poets and their ways of knowledge that fell victim.

One of the greatest battlegrounds is in the text of Plato's *The Republic*. Bruce Lincoln has written,

> "In the network of communicative relations envisioned by Plato, poets—who understood themselves to mediate between gods and humans—were significantly repositioned. The space that he assigned to them is that which lies between the state and its lowliest subjects, where they craft mythoi, at the direction of philosopher kings for mothers and nurses to pass onto their charges." [31]

This was a re-evaluation of myth that would be taken up by future intellectuals with enormous and long lasting impact. Plato positioned myth and reason as opposites, which was a great strategy for promoting of the role of the philosophers, shaped in his own mold.

So we live in a world where the dominant discourse presents this great block, this impediment, which is the enthroning of empirical scientific knowledge as the only true way of knowledge: that the rest is just making stuff up, entertainment, fantasy, fiction, delusion, etc.. So, to break through that, we must give value and credence to these other ways of knowledge, that which the Irish called *imbas*, the Welsh *awen* and Other ways of knowing[32] They may come from trance and other visionary states, even from plants that are forbidden by our legal strictures.

Many are the techniques of gnosis. With them we find the keys to unlock the iron cage that Max Weber saw we'd been put in. Better still, they are the reagent for the dissolution of the steel-like shell that our modern belief systems have encased us in, It can start to dissolve—if this can be painful, it's because it's so deeply a part of modern westerners and we have been impaired. Let us slip shell-less into the night and encounter the enchanted world that still lies around us, even though we had been blind to it before. What better language than that of myth to communicate it to others? And what better way to talk about animist relationality, anyway?

The enchanted world is the animist world, where humans are but one type of person in vast nets and tangles of persons: animal, plant, even mineral, and gods too.

"Animists are people who recognize that the world is full of persons, only some of whom are human, and that life is always lived in relationship with others," writes Graham Harvey. *"Persons are beings, rather than objects, who are animated and social towards others (even if they are not always sociable)."*[33]

Animist practice involves living respectfully with these other beings, obvious to us, or not.

There was a woman who married a bear, there was a man who married a selkie, there was...

And the salmon people wonder why their bones are no longer returned to the water, and plant persons wonder why they are no longer gathered...

There is a eucalyptus stand down the way where the spirits message me....

Mythic tales sprout everywhere even on concrete walls, and run like rhizomes and electricity through worlds revivified. When someone(s) calls out, we will stop trying to pretend it didn't happen.

In the 19th century the poet Friedrich Schiller used the term '*die entgotterung der Natur*', the degodding of nature for the process of disenchantment; in our communal practices of reenchantment nature appears engodded once again. May more and more of us once again hear and take heed of the songs of the enchanted garden, until the dead grey world of disenchantment falls away like a cobweb in a rising wind. •

Finchuill

is a Celtic Reconstructionist fili, a Druid, a mystes of Antinous (Ekklesía Antínoou), a queer polytheist at large, and an animist. Finnchuill writes for Air N-Aithesc: A Celtic Reconstructionist Peer Reviewed Magazine, is the author of From The Prow of Myth (a book of devotional poetry), and blogs at Finnchuillsmast at wordpress.

---

31   (Lincoln, 42)

32   According to Celticist, Nora Chadwick, empirical knowledge, *sous*, was distinguished from revealed knowledge, *fius* (*Poetry and Prophecy*).

---

33   (Harvey, xi)

The Winter Of Our World

Call To The Cold Gods

(Judith O'Grady)

The Dark Half of the Year, Hallowe'e'n to May-day, is ruled by the Gods of Winter. I think of Them as the Yew King, His advisor and strategist the Calleach Beara (aka: the Blue Hag), and His battle leader the Holly Warrior. At the beginning of the season, the Calleach bangs Her staff on the ground to freeze it and end growth. In the dormant period She creates, the Yew King battles for supremacy over Summer. As well as leading Winter's troops—storm, cold, ice, snow—the Holly Warrior heads up the Yule festivities as Fool. The King dies after the Longest Night but the Holly Warrior and the troops fight on desperately, creating February, the terrible month.

The Gods of the Dark Half are intimidating because They don't really care for humans. They are coldly uncaring—the cold of deep ice, bare stone, and season-deep snow. In Their world, all actions lead to results and *I'm sorry* or *that wasn't what I meant* cannot turn aside the outcome.

We have messed up our world, and we will reap that harvest. Not the golden, ricks-of-hay and Harvest-Home Festival but the one we grew in acres of shanty-towns and slave-factories, the one coughed out of our smoke-spewing cars, airplanes, and monster trucks, the one born from the hunger of many and the waste of a few.

What can we do? We are, of course, *very sorry* but that doesn't right anything at all. We can point to our tiny-ness —we ourselves have made so little of the general mess and we alone can do so little to pick it up. Perhaps it is time to call in the Great Judges, Pitiless and Un-Merciful as They are, to pass the sentence on humankind.

Many times I have found in conversation an anthropocentric bias that would be funny if it wasn't also a part of the problem. I will be talking to what I call 'World-Enders' who all have a favorite scenario:

"We will run out of oil and the world will end....."

"Ebola will mutate to aerosol and the world will end...."

"The oceans will die and the world will end....."

When I point out that people will die or be inconvenienced or have trouble but the World will carry on, people-less and perhaps better off in the long run, they are shocked and struggle to re-phrase the World-End in a way that is accurate but still conveys (to their mind) the absoluteness and gravity of the problem. This, sadly, results in an ear-worm (as we know it) and still leaves them and me on two sides of perception.

Earth has weathered many storms, comets, and die-offs and She is still here.

Everyone has seen that time-line—the formation of the planet is the start, the beginning of soupy life is here, dinosaurs are way along here, proto-humans, etc., were just seconds ago. Or something like that. It could be that we are the failed experiment and Earth will gradually subsume our non-biodegradable waste down into the magma and let something else unroll from what's left. I believe that we have an undeniable place—we are the different animals. In my ultra-Polytheistic and Animist belief system, the other animals (besides ourselves, that is) and the rocks, lakes, trees, mountains, river systems (you get the picture) all speak to the Gods reflexively, without having to try.

We alone struggle to open lines of communication with the Gods (and all those other things as well), and with this struggle we engage in a different level of free will and choice when the Gods and we speak. I believe that this different-ness of communication is important to the Gods; I do not know why the Gods value stubbornness and incomprehension, but it seems clear that They do.

But we are not the only hope of the Gods and Earth; if necessary They will stir around and try out Dolphins or Elephants with a God-Speaker in their brains. Or some life-form unimaginable to us, formulated much later on in that previously mentioned time-line of the World.

What we can do, after feeling *very sorry*, is try in good faith to take one forward step. By ourselves if necessary, in collaboration with other well-meaning people, communicating with and aiding the Spirits of the World by picking trash and cleaning water-ways. By sharing and caring, we may be able to live through the adjudication of the Gods.•

Judith O'Grady

Judith is an elderly Druid (Elders are trees, neh?) living on a tiny urban farm in Ottawa, Canada. She speaks respectfully to the Spirits, shares her home and environs with insects and animals, and fervently preaches ungrassing yards and repurposing trash (aka 'found-object art'). She is also the author of "God-Speaking," from Moon Books

The Year of Dark Epiphanies

Explorations of Death and the Divine

(Margaret Killjoy)

Greece wasn't really, technically, on fire. Most of it was just falling apart. This was 2011, and austerity measures had been hard at work for a few years already, gutting the economy, destroying lives, and driving half the population to xenophobia. There were a lot of anarchists in prison there, at that time. Well, always. But I was paying extra attention to it just then because I was on a ferry from Italy, heading to Greece for the first time in my life

It was a year of dark epiphanies, a year during which I wrapped my head around a lot of adult, scary bullshit. It was the year I put the words "anxiety" and "panic" to the demon that'd been plaguing my brain. It was the year I realized that actions have consequences beyond immediate and physical ones like getting arrested or injured or sick. It was the year I started to grapple with the divine, death, and family.

I spent two days and a night on the floor of the deck with the other people who don't have the money for cabins. I watched the Mediterranean go by and tried not to terrify myself with what the Greek border guards might make of me.

"Fuck," I said to myself, hopefully sub-vocally, "I wish I believed in God."

To know the divine is one way to gain the strength to move past fear. It would be a lot easier to have that comfort to fall back on.

I wondered for awhile if it's possible to wage war without faith. Faith in God is probably the common type, but I bet the hordes of godless communists and anarchists who fought fascism in the 20th century had faith of another sort.

The anarchist martyr August Spies (d. 1887) stood on the gallows and shouted: "the day will come when our silence will be more powerful than the voices you strangle today." That's a kind of faith.

He was right, what's more. The martyrdom of him and his four compatriots spurred a national discussion of labor issues and won a great number of people over to anarchism. His grave in Chicago is, ironically, a federally-recognized landmark.

I do have faith. I believe in anarchism—I believe that freedom is a relationship between people, not something doled out by a state or a church or something that springs forth from our wallets. I believe it's worth fighting for that freedom, even if it scares the living shit out of me to stand up to cops and jailers and all of their ilk. I believe that these ideals, these relationships of freedom we forge in life, will survive my passing.

But on that ferry, I just wished I believed in God. It seemed a simpler way to accept mortality.

The ferry landed, and I got into the country without a hitch. I stumbled my way through a month or so of trying to be useful to the people I care about and the global movement I love. To be frank I'm not sure I had much success at either.

Tradition is a myth, a story we tell each other. 364 days and 23 hours of the year, I despise Christmas music. When I'm with the family I rarely see, at the darkest time of year with the cold about to set in, I understand it. "We've grown a little older, we've grown a little colder," goes one chorus.

My immediate family is getting older without a younger generation taking its place, and my extended family seems to be drifting apart. We're Catholic—culturally at least—and it's only at Christmas that I see more than a few of my relatives. Christmas Eve has never been the same since my father's parents died. We get together at the same house, eat the same food, sing the same songs, and it isn't the same.

Tradition, in a conservative sense, clings to a fictitious, static way of being. Nothing stays the same in this world. The rapid pace of technological development and population growth in the modern era makes the inevitability of change readily apparent, but I believe with all my heart that the environment and the ways of life we develop to interact with that environment have always shifted from generation to generation. The conservative understanding of tradition is a violent lie we tell one another to force conformity to an illusory ideal.

At its best, tradition is a buoy in the chaotic and metaphorical sea of time. It signals the way to shore or at least gives us

> *I do have faith. I believe in anarchism—I believe that freedom is a relationship between people, not something doled out by a state or a church or something that springs forth from our wallets. I believe it's worth fighting for that freedom, even if it scares the living shit out of me to stand up to cops and jailers and all of their ilk.*

something to cling to so as to catch our breath. We are not beholden to tradition. It doesn't confine us, it doesn't trap us in the past. I'll call this the liberatory interpretation of tradition mostly because I like the word liberatory (a word which doesn't exist even though my friends use it all the damn time).

Since no one has ever had much luck forcing me to conform to anything, I've never personally been much affected by the conservative understanding of tradition. I've never presumed to do what my family says ought to be done. But it took me until the year of dark epiphanies to appreciate the liberatory version.

Winter holidays are the vain and beautiful attempt to drive back the sorrow of aging.

It doesn't work, in the end, but of course in the end the dark and the cold come for us all.

The men in my family drift in that liminal space between paganism and Catholicism. One winter, one of them said to me: "the reason I like Catholicism is that it's essentially polytheistic. We revere the saints, each a different aspect of the divine." Well, I paraphrase him. The next year, he declared he was a pagan. He calls me on winter solstice, sometimes, to wish me a happy new year's. It warms my heart.

Another dark year, anxiety was doing its best to destroy me. Chest pains, numbness in my limbs and jaw, headaches, and every morning I was wracked with hot and cold flashes for hours at a go. It wasn't that I wanted to die, it was that I knew I was about to.

"You have a guardian angel," my family told me.

My grandfather was Catholic, probably wasn't very pagan. He designed ships for the navy, and once they were built he'd make the captain drive them into the worst storms they could find. Safety testing. He stood out on the deck and let the wind and the rain and the waves try to tear apart these ships he'd designed. According to my family, the same divine creature watches over me as watched over him.

It's easy to poke holes in this. But when I want to be brave, sometimes I think about my granddad on one of his ships.

People are up in arms about how the word "literally" can now, according to the dictionary, be accurately used to mean "figuratively." People think this is literally the worst thing ever. This never bothered me, personally. I actually thought it was kind of cool to have an expression of hyperbole so strong it says "this isn't even hyperbole."

When I think about a literal understanding of the divine, this ambiguous meaning is perfect. My granddad literally had this invisible dude (not God, a minor dude in the invisible pantheon) watching his back who kept him from drowning. When I say literally, I mean figuratively but he meant literally. But it's the same word because it's the same thing, in the end.

It's a shame about what happens when people take their literal gods too literally of course, and start denying that the other people's literal gods exist. And for all my newfound acceptance of my upbringing, I think it's outright monstrous to tell a child that if they don't behave they'll be tortured for all eternity. But the evidence against every religion that's ever held power is clearcut and well-documented, unnecessary to explore herein.

Near the end of that dark year, I developed a faith, of sorts. It's one of the mix-mashed things that takes a reverence for the universe and throws some metaphorical (literal!) gods on top. I'm old enough now that I'm willing to accept that I'm culturally Catholic, but it would be just as honest to call myself an atheist as a pagan. If religion is a metaphor to help us make sense of the fact that we're skeletons inhabited by colonies of microbes and stitched together with bloody meat, then I figured I could use one. I'd be a chaos magician who doesn't believe in magic.

My fabricated faith doesn't do shit for my anxiety. I tried for awhile. I had this mantra: "I am of the earth. I will return to the earth." I said it to myself as panic came over me in waves, and to be real, it didn't work. A darker epiphany still: I gave it all this thought, but religion wasn't enough.

It's been mostly the detached, scientific Cognitive Behavioral Therapy—and the tools it taught me—that's gotten me through. As the worst things in my life happen, I go to self-diagnosis mode: how am I feeling, concretely? On an emotional pain scale of 1 to 10, where am I? Where do I think it would appropriate to be? How long does each wave of panic or grief take hold of my mind? How long are the intervals between?

Those are the kinds of questions that work for me. Better than invisible dudes or nature-is-god or even freedom-and-anarchy-are-all-that-matter.

But coming to know the divine, in my own way, has helped me understand the bigger picture. It's helped me come to terms with the arc of my life, of the role I play as a strand in the woven twine of my family, my movement, and human history. I feel more connected to the earth, I feel more comfortable with the inevitability of my own death.

All light comes from darkness, after all.

Margaret Killjoy

is an author and editor who travels with no fixed home. Margaret's most recent book is A Country of Ghosts, a utopian novel published by Combustion Books in 2014.

Restoring Life to Death

(Sean Donahue)

There is death. And then there is death.

Salmon swim upstream to spawn, and then die, having exerted themselves completely. Eagles and bears drag salmon carcasses into the forest, and the remnants nourish the trees. Without the salmon, the rainforest where I live would not exist. Salmon runs were and are vitally important times in the calendars of Coast Salish peoples all along the north Pacific coast.

My Irish and Scottish ancestors were salmon people too, and there was a time when salmon bodies nourished their forests as well. Salmon were associated with knowledge, wisdom, and initiation.

Salmon face death on their own terms. Like sacred kings, their bodies and their blood nourish the land. In the eyes of the forest, in the eyes of the people who inhabit it, in the eyes of eagle and raven and bear, and in the eyes of the gods, their deaths are right and good and life-giving.

But this year in the Columbia River and its tributaries, more than half of the Sockeye run has died before reaching its ancestral spawning grounds. Fisheries biologists cite warm temperatures and low water levels, the result of a hot, dry season when the rainforest has barely seen any rain. Many First Nations are shutting down Sockeye fishing, despite the cost to tradition and to food security.

These death of the salmon before they can spawn is a different kind of death.

My death gods come to me in the form of a bear and an old woman with Datura blossoms in her long, white hair. They have always been the most tender and loving of gods to me, despite their reputation for ferocity.

When a student of mine died in a fire, they helped me open the gate to allow her to pass through to the otherworld, and, though her death hurt deeply, they showed that it was in the flow of all things—in ways that my talking, thinking self still can't fully understand. When I knelt in the dirt rubbing Devil's Club tincture into the gums of a horse, trying to revive him, they let me keep the gate jammed shut until I knew all hope was lost, and then led his spirit bounding through to the other side.

It makes sense that such gods would be companions to an herbalist. Herbalist Stephen Buhner once told me that a healer needs to know intimacy with death. Otherwise, we cannot walk beside people in fear and pain and surrender.

An intimacy with death gods has taught me that not all deaths are the same in their eyes. Some deaths are not in the flow of things.

My gods show me the deaths of unarmed Black and Brown and Indigenous people murdered by police. And the murders of Black, Brown, and Indigenous people, so many of them women, so many of them Trans, that the police refuse to investigate.

They show me the Iraqi children who died of dysentery and cholera when the U.S. bombed Iraq's water and sewage treatment plants and then refused to allow their repair or the importation of adequate antibiotics for well over a decade.

They show me the caribou drowned when rivers were dammed.

My gods tell me that while they carried these dead out of this world, their true place remains within it.

These dead are restless, rattling at the gates.

In 2001, in Colombia, I met Hector Mondragon, an economist who was tortured for his support for striking oil workers and then refused to give the names of his torturers to guerrillas who wanted to avenge him. Over several decades of work with unions, Indigenous, and campesino groups, many of his friends were killed by his country's armed factions. Hector said, "My murdered compañeros were killed twice . . ." once by bullets or machetes or bombs, and once by a world that refused to acknowledge their lives and their deaths.

Global capitalism was born of primitive accumulation — the violent enclosure (theft and privatization) of land, material, and labor from the Indigenous cultures of Europe, Africa, Asia, and the Americas which stoked its fires. Today, that process of accumulation continues around the world, from the rise in prison labor to gentrification to the commodification of water to sweatshop labor in Bangladesh to the violation of Indigenous sovereignty in the service of Canada's fossil fuel "resource economy." (And as writer Fjothr Lokakvan reminded me, the bodies of ancient dead things, in the form of oil and gas, are literally the fuel that drives the engines of capitalism.)

The culture that arises from capitalism conceals the bodies of the dead — ancient, historical, and modern; human and non-human — so that its members can be insulated from the bloody cost of their standard of living. The erasure of the memory of so many lives and deaths is like a continuous pouring of concrete to prevent the return of what was driven from this world.

But some of us remember— and that makes the concrete begin to crack.

On the morning of the second day of Many Gods West, a Polytheist Conference in Olympia, Washington, I was spirited away to Tumwater Falls.

Standing on a bridge over the Deschutes River, my companion and I looked down at what had been a rushing waterfall in seasons past. Rocks once covered with water were laid bare, and a spray that would have misted us in another time barely made it a quarter of the way up to the bridge. I looked at the withering vegetation on its banks and saw a wasteland expanding for want of any willing to ask the perilous question.

My green-eyed forest-hearted companion began to speak to me about witnessing — about how when we truly see each other and truly see a river and truly see a tree, it calls forth something luminous and alive from within them. My heart softened and my perspective shifted. I began to see the bare stones in their smooth, fluid beauty. The land and the water began to make themselves known to me.

That night, in ritual, I would meet Cathobodua, a Gaulish war goddess whose name and image had been forgotten for centuries, and accept the blessing of her warrior's mark. The next night I met the Matronae, the forgotten mothers of my ancestors, and recommitted myself to the return of what was driven from this world that is essential to its survival.

Witnessing and remembering are the beginning of restoring sacredness to the death around us to enable it to feed new life.

The Greek poet, Dinos Christianopolous wrote:

what didn't you do to bury me

but you forgot I was a seed.

When the seeds contained in the memory of the dead are able to break through the concrete, we shall see what this world can grow.

Sean Donahue

is an herbalist, poet, witch, and feral creature living on unceded WSANEC territory on the southern tip of what colonial cartographers now call Vancouver Island. He worked as a political organizer for a decade or so before realizing an introvert with a decidedly non-linear approach to the world was better suited to talking with plants and gods than to managing organizations, and also had a brief career as a journalist reporting on repression and resistance in Latin America. He is Priest and a keeper of the Green Wand in the BlackHeart Line of the Anderson Feri Tradition of Witchcraft. He blogs at greenmanramblings.blogspot.com/

Contemplating the Ruins & Reviving Mythic Stories
(Pegi Eyers)

"Our Ancestors experienced life in terms of imagination and intuition, and this mythic worldview has value for us today. A new interest is awakening in primal mind, fantasies and dreams. We have the need to relate back to a deeper level of life which is more direct and full of feeling, with a natural grace and wisdom that is more appealing than all the dazzling accomplishments of the intellectual ego. Myth has once again become important."

"When the stories a society shares are out of tune with its circumstances, they can become self-limiting, even a threat to survival. This is our current situation."

In these last days of Empire, the "endless growth" agenda of eco-fascism, economic hegemony and corporatocracy is dissolving, falling apart under the weight of unsustainability, and a groundswell of people from all walks of life are moving away from these delusional and insane systems. The paradigm of humanity as lord and master of *Mother Earth* has run its course, and it is becoming harder and harder to believe in the fallacy of a mechanical universe and our separation from the natural world. *"We are living at a time in which the old story of domination and control has lost its power, and we are in a liminal, in-between time, still searching for a new story."*

At this point in history, it would seem highly apropos to reject the human-centric and hubristic notions that human beings are a "God Species" who rule the world, that more and better technology will solve the problems that technology created in the first place, or that continued "progress" is the only way forward. That the colonial dream would have been adopted planet-wide was perhaps something the early "meme spreaders"[34] did not foresee, but the Earth clearly cannot sustain billions of people living at the height of civilizational benefit and luxury. "*Unless you believe infinite growth is possible on a finite planet*"[35] it is time to redefine our paradigm and adopt a different mythic story for self, community and the world, to return to the values of interexistence and a respect for natural law.

The conveniences, communication devices and media bombardment of our high-mobility modern lifestyle have given us the illusion that human beings are the center of the universe. Our addiction to entertainment and diversion, the ongoing incestuous interaction with our emotional dramas and human inventions—to the exclusion of all other life on Earth—is narcissistic, dysfunctional and immoral. What spell have we been under? Thinking that human endeavors and human-centric concerns are the only ones that matter keeps us trapped in the sinkhole of modernism, contributes to the ideology of Empire, and does nothing to return us to right relationship with the land. Unlearning the habits of civilization means rejecting the domestication we have adopted from techno-industrial society in favor of earth-wise Pagan skills, returning to the rich matrix of indigenous mind, and learning how to be "true human beings" once again.

We need the vision of an earth-rooted paradigm to counteract Empire's mandate to devour the earth's resources and spirit. Experiencing, creating and believing both ancient and new narratives that honor and celebrate the natural world (and our place within it) are urgently needed to bend the curve. Based on the *Old Ways*, we need to tell revived stories about ourselves, reclaimed eco-myths to guide us forward, and rejuvenated manifestos that celebrate our integration

We need the vision of an earth-rooted paradigm to counteract Empire's mandate to devour the earth's resources and spirit

with the natural world. Our archaic spirit needs to rise again in a weaving of timeless stories of growth, regeneration, rites of passage, energy, motion, illumination, magic, decay, and all the earth's processes that dwell both in us and the other-than-human-world.

Mirroring the "new myth" in full interaction with others is both a spiritual and political act that will disrupt the business-as-usual of Empire in ways we can only imagine. Diverse human groups worldwide have always used mythic stories to record our most sacred origins, to hold the keystone beliefs, cultural meanings, values and destinies specific to each society. Creation stories (or accounts of how our particular social order came into being), along with explanations and exemplars, are human attempts to answer the most fundamental questions of existence and form the building blocks of a collective reality. Arising from both the intellect and the imagination, narrative epics and parables are "lessons for living" that offer us guidance for navigating both the inner and outer worlds.

Keystone stories and important events in history are transferred from one generation to the next, and are integrated in rituals and ceremonies that include the bardic arts, entertainment, music, songs, call-and-response, poetry, dancing and drumming. Throughout history, pagan peoples have relied on the story-keepers to maintain the tribal records, to continue the richness of history, identity and culture. By reaching back to ancestral knowledge, conveying teachings or validating the prestige and responsibilities of tribal members, each storyteller brings with them a unique piece of the mythic puzzle. The oral transmission of collective memories becomes a living worldview that keeps the cultural traditions of the group alive.

Focused on interspecies communication and our soul connections to the other-than-human world, our shared stories can outline our rapport with other beings and the realm of the shapeshifters. The natural world is the entry point to the "dreamtime," a place where our access to soul expressions and personal mythology merge. "*Stories and their ceremonies weave our world together: the story of corn maiden and mother, of salmon's death and rebirth, of bear's human wife, of coyote's foul tricks and lynx's loneliness. These stories of ecological conscience are a council where the voices of all species may be heard. It is through these stories that the Earth can be restored, for these eco-*

---

34. Daniel Quinn calls the foundational worldviews of culture "memes." Daniel Quinn, *Beyond Civilization: Humanity's Next Great Adventure*, Broadway, 2000

35Charles Eisenstein, *A New Story of the People*, TEDxWhitechapel video, February 13, 2013: (www.youtube.com/watch?v=Mj0xh4c2Dj0)

narratives are an 'ilbal', a 'seeing instrument'. Looking through the eyes of others as their stories are told, we may hear and understand the voices of our relatives."[36]

An important purpose for our ongoing oral history is to outline the interactions and lived experiences that arise from our essential bond to *Earth Community*, to recount the stories that are held within geographical locations on the land. Whether at key points like sacred sites or more personal lived places, the storied landscape brings our lore to life—the earth deities, Gods, Goddesses or sages we honor, the creatures we dream about, and the paradoxes we cannot explain.

For a powerful example of the oral tradition as a living worldview, we can look to the life of the great Okanagan storyteller and orator Harry Robinson, who was wholly immersed in the natural world in every waking moment. During the transcribing of his priceless story-cycles, scholar Wendy Wickwire noted that:

> "Harry travelled to Vancouver to undergo medical treatment under the care of an elderly Chinese herbalist. Only then did the depth of Harry's mythological world become truly apparent. As we passed through downtown Vancouver on his visits to the doctor, I realized that all the traffic lights and cars meant nothing to Harry. They were almost an abstraction, an interesting but fleeting diversion from the timeless real world of Coyote, Fox and Owl."[37]

In our own process to reject the failed experiment of industrial civilization, connect deeply to the land and embody the brilliant mythology of our own ancestral knowledge, can we also have no doubt that entering urban space is an illusion and an aberration, an insult to ourselves, the Earth and Her many creatures and elements? Can we too contemplate the ruins of Empire and see it as an abstraction, a fleeting diversion that for a long and unmerciful time tried to demonize Gaia and

separate us from our one true home? As we examine our own life story within the context of Empire-building, we need to deconstruct the experiences that do not serve us, and reclaim the kinship model of our relationship to the wild.

To re-indigenize ourselves means re-inhabiting our local ecosystems, and returning to the various features and creatures in the bioregional landbase that inform and inspire. Developing eco-mythic literacy means unlearning the consensual worldview of Empire in favor of older ways to see the world, to think and feel our way into a re-landed perspective with storytelling, ceremonies, intuitive workings and sacred art. Our creative, mystic, and eco-poetic abilities will blossom again when we dwell in a sense of oneness with the natural world, and we gain new wisdom when we are living as a part of (rather than apart from) the *Web of All Life*. A keen knowledge of the surrounding ecosystem is fundamental to a deep sense of interconnection and is imperative to a sustainable future, and communicating this eco-literacy to others, especially children, is the most important task we face.

"Stories nurture our connection to place and to each other. They show us where we have been and where we can go. They remind us of how to be human, and how to live alongside the other lives that animate this planet."[38]

So, what are the new Earth Stories? In addition to narratives that arise from our localized re-landing, these thoughts and "chapters" may be a good beginning:

we need to deconstruct the experiences that do not serve us, and reclaim the kinship model of our relationship to the wild

- To return to our pre-colonial Paganism or indigenity knowing we are all children of Earth, and that our place is within, not above, the circle of creation,
- To reorient our consciousness toward a more integral relationship with the Earth,
- To move toward a paradigm shift that includes the land and the other-than-human world,
- To look to nature as a knowledgeable and inspiring teacher, as Gaia herself provides us with the stories for a new era,

36Joan Halifax, *The Fruitful Darkness: Reconnecting with the Body of the Earth*, Harper Collins, 1993

37*Write it on Your Heart: The Epic World of an Okanagan Storyteller*, by Harry Robinson and Wendy Wickwire (editor), Talonbooks, 1989. From the first of three volumes, the stories of Harry Robinson (Interior Salish, Lower Similkameen Band, B.C.) were collected by Wendy Wickwire. While working on her doctoral thesis, she recognized in Harry Robinson what Thomas King (Cherokee) would describe as "*the most powerful storytelling voice in North America.*"

38 Susan J. Tweit, *Walking Nature Home: A Life's Journey*, University of Texas Press, 2009

- To address ecological solutions that maintain and improve the health of natural systems and the diversity of all life,

- To revive and embrace the natural law of species diversity in a multiplicity of ethnicities, belief systems, partnerships, unique societies and Earth communities,

- To revalue our bodies, the dignity of materiality, and working with our hands,

- To live each day as a sacred act,

- To love the land as central to our most cherished dreams and memories, to care for and restore the Earth, and

- To take a stand for ecological defence.

The human mind is as much a part of nature as a boreal forest, and the imaginal states of dreaming, imagining, wandering in nature, making magic and creating mythologies is key. In times of massive change and transition, sharing and collaborating with our kindred spirits and communities on old/new ecocentric stories is an integral part of reclaiming our primitivist, animist, Pagan, Neo-Pagan or re-constructionist paths. Human beings have a role to play as earth protectors and earth keepers, and our challenge is to honor each other, all beings, and the earth as *Sacred*. Reframing and rewriting our own stories where we find ourselves right now —in the ruins of Empire – will automatically reconnect us to the mythic realms of spirit, and will enlarge our transformation to knowing that we belong to the Earth. When your thoughts and actions go beyond the narrow confines of your individualistic concerns and revolve around the land and the welfare of the whole, you are well on your way to becoming a "true human being!" In these times of cataclysmic return, the "new myth" is the same one already in place that humanity has had for millennia, imbedded in worldview(s) that respect the human place within the circle of creation, and that express our overwhelming love for *Earth Community*.

Pegi Eyers

Author of "Ancient Spirit Rising: Reclaiming Your Roots & Restoring Earth Community," Pegi Eyers is occupied with challenging worldviews, contributing to the paradigm shift and working with the decolonization process in herself and others. A Celtic Animist who sees the world through a spiritual lens, she is a devotee of nature-based culture and all that is sacred to the Earth. Pegi Eyers is an advocate for our interconnection with Earth Community and the recovery of authentic ancestral wisdom and traditions for all people. She lives in the countryside on the outskirts of Nogojiwanong in Mississauga Anishnaabe territory (Peterborough, Ontario, Canada) on a hilltop with views reaching for miles in all directions. www.stonecirclepress.com

Mysterium Tremendum
(Christopher Scott Thompson)

1

Hot ashes sizzle on the rocks and snow
While high above me, hunting falcons glide.
A single strand of grayish smoke still curls
Like twisting rope against a huge, white sky
So cold it shocks the last thin threads of dream
And leaves me clean and startled and awake,
Though cold, and frightened by my coldness too.
The foothills stretch behind me, nearly bare,
But pocked with lonely, black-white scrubs and birch,
And broken here and there by boulders too
Like naked hands that grasp the empty skies.
I pour a stream of steaming water out,
And orange coals go black with veins of fire,
Then fade to gray. I heft my leather pack,
Which holds a bare few odds and ends, and stand.
This land is haunted by a howling wind,
That whistles like a steam train through the hills
Then blasts across the white and empty plains
And drives a cloud of snowdust, thin and dry
And glittering like shards of ground-up glass
Through barren branches. Though the road is long,
There's nothing to be gained by staying here.

2

The white light fades. And all around, the wind
Seems hushed for just a moment. Then it roars.
A sheet of crystal dust springs up and roams
Half-drunkenly from hill to hill. I stand

With eyes cast down, and feel the hostile kiss
Of ice against my face. I look again
And find myself alone. My heart is bleak
With such a wind as this. I face the path
As if its outline mapped the wasted track
Of all my years. But then I shrug, and walk.
The hard, bright snow that breaks beneath my boot
Shines white as distant galaxies. The storm,
As predatory as those passing birds
Seems somehow not to touch me. I am dead,
And wrapped in distance like a shroud. The world
Must have its reasons, but my reason fails.
I set my face against the harsh, white scream
Of primal winter, and set forth again.
Through spiral clouds of wind and shards of ice
Like shattered glass, my solitary path
Is marked behind me by the shape of boots,
Ahead of me by nothing. In this wind,
My thoughts themselves seem hushed, then torn away.

3

The path ahead is packed, hard, crusted snow
Through which a single, withered clump of grass
Pokes up its pale green head. The air seems clean
And charged with life like static, and I breathe
A lung full as my feet break through the ice
To sink into the snow beneath. Ahead,
A wrathful, orange sky. The clouds, like thoughts,
Change constantly and pass. And in their train
Ride intimations of a flood of ghosts.
Before me stands a circle made of stones,
An ancient holy place once sanctified
By blood and fire, now by wind and time.
Nine stones in all, nine gray and twisted stones
Nine long forgotten, cold, ice-crusted stones.
This place is of the Other, and the face
Of utter silence shines behind and through
Like shifting lights behind a veil. I kneel.
Mysterium Tremendum, how your great
And awful gnosis penetrates my being!
In such a place as this the changing years
Are all retained at once. My heart is still

Before the fearful mystery I've found.
In hushed yet pregnant reverence, I breathe
The magic in from every silent rock
And frozen pool of water, and I know -
A god is here behind the rock and ice.
The gods are here, and we are not alone.

4

It's time to drink the clear, cold wine of dream
Directly from the source, and know its tang
As well as any ancient poet knew
The flavor of the dawn songs of the world.
Our bards have drained the wells of story dry
In singing odes to nymphs they never knew
Except through pages in a well-worn book -
And now no longer sing of nymphs at all.
Our priests have done the same with every creed
They once assured would save us from ourselves.
Our scientists have chopped up every truth
In bloody chunks of fact, and then announced
That all they found was meat. The world is dead
Because we chose to kill it. But the gods -
The gods are here, and we are not alone.
Real magic's not a thing you go to learn
In books of lore like dried-out yellow bones.
It's not a thing that you can get in school
By sitting at the feet of wise old men
And letting them dissect the things you've read
To make a mess of symbols. Myth is awe!
Real myth will leave you shaking on the ground
In love with every speck of earth, alive,
And all alive with you. It's time to rise
In holy rage and wreath your head in lights
You've plucked yourself until your eyes, ablaze,
Illuminate the world. It's time to learn
New myths directly from the land of dreams
And plant those myths like seeds in every rock,
In every rushing stream, in every hill,
In every city, till the whole world blooms,
Until the whole world comes alive again.

Christopher Scott Thompson

is a writer and historical swordsmanship instructor who lives in Maine with his family. He is the author of A God Who Makes Fire: The Bardic Mysticism of Amergin.

The Manifestation of the Unseen

Roy Cohn: What's it like? After?

Belize: After...?

Roy Cohn: This misery ends?

Belize: Hell or heaven?

Roy Cohn: [laughs]

Belize: Like San Francisco.

Roy Cohn: A city! Good! I was worried... it'd be a garden. I hate that shit.

Belize: Mmmm. Big city. Overgrown with weeds, but flowering weeds. On every corner a wrecking crew and something new and crooked going up catty corner to that. Windows missing in every edifice like broken teeth, gritty wind, and a gray high sky full of ravens.

Roy Cohn: Isaiah.

Belize: Prophet birds, Roy. Piles of trash, but lapidary like rubies and obsidian, and diamond-colored cowspit streamers in the wind. And voting booths. And everyone in Balenciaga gowns with red corsages, and big dance palaces full of music and lights and racial impurity and gender confusion. And all the deities are creole, mulatto, brown as the mouths of rivers. Race, taste and history finally overcome. And you ain't there.

Roy Cohn: And Heaven?

Belize: That was Heaven, Roy.[39]

The Matter of the Gods

(Jonathan Woolley)

MANY GODS; BEYOND BELIEF?

There is something strange happening within Paganism. It is strange not because it is unexpected—indeed, all families of religions go through it at one time or another—nor because it is unusual—indeed, its like happens all the time. What is strange about it, is that it seems to run contrary to the social circumstances of Paganism today. Indeed, given our highly networked and increasingly virtual world, and the relatively small size of the Pagan community (small, even when compared to the number of Pagans who don't "do" the Pagan community, but are solitary), it seems quite remarkable.

Paganism is diverging.

In America, we are witnessing the ascent of a new kind of hard polytheism. The familiar refrains of Gaia-theorists, duotheist Wiccans, archetype-channelers, and feminist Mono-theaists are now joined by the carousing of a bunch of upstarts. These contend that no, the gods are not all aspects, incarnations, or faces of The One (or The Two), that is Nature, or its Creator Goddess and her God. The gods are real, and distinctly so—each a person in their own right, just as we [humans] are, and that believing in them as Actually Extant Beings is, really, okay. These polytheists reject the slippery theorising documented by Tanya Luhrman's trailblazing ethnography[40], and the postmodern construction of experience-as-basically-subjective articulated by Sabina Magliocco[41]. The Gods, for the new polytheists, are Real.

---

39   Angels in America, Tony Kushner

40   Luhrmann, T. (1989) *Persuasions of the Witch's Craft: Ritual Magic in Contemporary England*. Cambridge, Mass.: Harvard University Press.

41   Magliocco, S. (2013) **Sabina Magliocco: Pagan Fundamentalism?** In *The Wild Hunt*. Available at http://wildhunt.org/2013/02/sabina-magliocco-pagan-fundamentalism.html. Last accessed 13/09/2015.

In Europe I have seen a different trend. The same old order –in which the same gentle theologies held sway—is being complicated here too, but not by a radical call for belief in many gods. Rather, belief *itself* is being set aside. European Pagans increasingly do not identify as "religious" or "believers" per se. Rather, to them, Paganism is something that is lived through, crafted, cast, brewed, known—hewn from raw being itself. To talk of "believing in the gods" here seems inappropriate. The gods as we know them are real, but the question of *how* they are real is both an open one, and one that doesn't matter very much. They are like love, maths, or motion sickness; part of our world, part of our traditions and customs—in a way that makes what we might think about them, well, *purely academic*. Fun to discuss, certainly. A question for the philosophers, perhaps. But not important for defining what we do, and think. As the late (and much loved) author Terry Pratchett once said,

"*Most witches don't believe in gods. They know that the gods exist, of course. They even deal with them occasionally. But they don't believe in them. They know them too well. It would be like believing in the postman.*"[42]

The witches of Britain are, in my experience, much like those of Pratchett's Discworld. Why bother believing in something, if you *know* it exists.

Much of this could be put down to broader differences between European and American societies. Although American society has been shaken by the rise of the unaffiliated "nones", religious ideas and themes nonetheless hold tremendous power in the collective imaginaries of the American people. In Europe, however, religion itself is a highly discredited concept—exhausted by millennia of ecumenical strife, and bored by centuries of tame state churches, European peoples no longer see religious concepts as being especially meaningful or relevant. As such, Paganism has increasingly developed along lines that are cultural, aesthetic, or philosophical in nature, rather than expressly religious. Talk is not of setting up churches, temples, and monasteries; but villages, festivals, and campaign groups. Although the Druid Network did succeed in getting approved as a religious charity by the Charity Commission recently, this development was greeted with disapproval amongst the majority of the Druids I know—*Druidry*, as many said to me, *is not even a religion*. I cannot say for certain if this is a purely Druidic phenomenon, but there does appear to be evidence from across the continent that suggests a gradual transformation of Paganism from a "religious" phenomenon, into a broader "cultural" one that is anything but "fundamentalist" – whether or not we look to socially progressive Asatru of Iceland, or the nature spirituality of atheistic Estonia.

Making sense, out of Chaos, out of Order

It might be imagined that these changes are pulling in opposite directions—the American trend reflecting a "radicalisation" of religious doctrine in the form of polytheism, while the European trend representing the fulfillment of the secu-

42   Pratchett, T. (1991) *Witches Abroad*. Victor Gollancz: London.

larisation thesis. I would disagree with this characterisation. To my mind, these trends have far more in common than might appear at first glance.

If we consider the old theological consensus, what becomes readily apparent is that in many respects, it really isn't too far removed from the spiritual conventions of the Western world's established religious orthodoxy. Pantheism and Panentheism have a vibrant life outside of Paganism, and the Goddess has her anchorites even within Christianity and Judaism. Even the duotheism of Wicca arguably puts very little clear water between itself and the distributed godhead of Christianity; instead of a Holy Trinity, we have a Holy Tryst. In short, from a theological standpoint, the first generations of Pagan writing owe far more to lay Catholicism and the New England Transcendentalists, than to anything recognisably pre-Christian.

However, what it did do was create a formal break with Christian and Jewish religious authority and the commitment to dogma that came with it. For 1500 years, the Christian Churches—be they Catholic, Orthodox, Protestant, or Restoration—held almost exclusive sway over the souls of Western Europeans; no spiritual life—save that of the oft-persecuted Jewish community —existed outside their universal purview. By creating a new category of spiritual expression that was officially outside both the Christian and Jewish communities, any mandatory requirement to fit with the creeds and customs laid down in Holy Scripture, Halakha or Canon Law was abolished. This was in itself startlingly radical; though the Enlightenment established the legitimacy of secular thought, it was the rise of new religious movements, including that of Paganism, that actively challenged the formal, ecclesiastical control of the spiritual realm.

In short; the first few generations of Pagan sages made a gateway through which forgotten beings, old souls, and the old ways could return to human society.

And that is exactly what is now taking place.

THE OLD WAYS, PLURAL

The crucial thing to remember is that what defined the old Paganism was explicitly *not* a single set of beliefs, nor a single set of customs. Europe, before the arrival of "the Nazarene" and his vision of the world, was a patchwork of different traditions, methods of enlightenment, esoteric systems, state cults, philosophies, and initiatory systems—all flourishing and fighting with one another, all very different in range and content. What united them—if anything—were cultural exchanges and political alliances that took place over time. The Druids, for example, commanded influence across tribal and linguistic boundaries in Iron Age Europe, just as Greek art, language and philosophy came to flourish across the Mediterranean during the same period. The Cultus of the Divine [Imperial] House united all who lived within the Roman Empire, just as various state-sponsored reverential traditions had forged civic or national identity prior to the Roman conquests.

Before the arrival of Christianity, a wide variety of interpretations of divinity existed—from the dualism of the gnostics, to the naturalism of the Stoics; from the pragmatic polytheism of the official cults to the mystical techniques advocated by Plotinus. When Christianity developed into a powerful force within Imperial politics, the drive to produce the Kingdom of Heaven on Earth became the new unifying ideology across the Roman world—an exclusive one, at that. Lacking any term to describe what they stood for, the opponents of this new order came to refer to the old ways as "Hellenism"; the defining attribute of which being a love of the Greek classical heritage that the Romans had inherited, and everything that had been syncretised with it. As Talal Asad has argued, before the rise of religion as a category, Christianity was once described as a *disciplina*—a system of government—just like that of the Empire itself[43]. The Christianisation was, then, the bringing of Imperial rule in line with the expectations of Christian discipline, at the expense of pre-Christian mores.

In a sense, what can be seen in the rise of The Church is a continuation of the process of conquest initiated by Rome itself. When Rome began, it was one political vision amongst many—the Capitoline Triad were just one constellation in a

Though the Enlightenment established the legitimacy of secular thought, it was the rise of new religious movements, including that of Paganism, that actively challenged the formal, ecclesiastical control of the spiritual realm.

---

43   Asad, T. (1993) *Genealogies of Religion.* Johns Hopkins Univ. Press: Baltimore.

myriad of political cults, spreading out from Alexandria to Bibracte and beyond. But as Roman rule became ever more absolute, the geopolitical reality of many peoples, each with their own moral, legal, and spiritual alliances faded away; being replaced by the singular authority of the Roman State. As the notion of this single *disciplina* became ever more established—manifest in the deification of the Roman State in the genius of the Emperors – it became possible to re-imagine the divine order in a way that better reflected what had been realized on Earth; a total system of control, focused upon a single authority. Christianity, with its emphasis upon one God and an absence of idols, was the perfect theological companion to this new arrangement. The fact that the unstable bricolage of Hellenism failed to halt the Christian advance is not at issue here: what is interesting is that the term adopted by the proponents of a non-Christian influence was linked to a loosely-organised cultural assemblage—Hellenism—that grew out of a long, mutual history of trade, war, and intellectual and ritual expression, and not a singular body of authoritative doctrine or law, laid down by a prophet and codified by his disciples.

> *Though what Pagans think and do is thoroughly contemporary, the fact that we're all doing it differently, in ways concordant with our particular contexts, is quintessentially pre-Christian.*

CONSTRUCTION, [RE]CONSTRUCTION

My analysis so far is heavily influenced by a school of thought—propounded by such scholars of religion as Talal Asad, S. N. Balagangadhara, and Timothy Fitzgerald—which argues that our contemporary concept of "religion" is highly specific to the context of modern, Western Christianity. Religion—as a separable sphere of life, concerned with spiritual beliefs, divinely-sanctioned morality, ritual, prayer, and mythology—is not a human universal. It is perfectly possible for spiritual life to exist in forms and varieties that look strikingly different to "religion", as that word is normally understood. Pre-Christian spiritual life in Europe—in all its bewildering diversity, contradiction, and creativity, inseparable from the rest of both public and private life—is a case in point. Indeed, it is arguable that the very fact that people define the spiritual so differently today—largely through the lens of "religion", rather than *disciplina* or anything else—means that it is impossible for us to posit any real substantive similarities between ancient and modern Paganisms.

But to my mind, the development of highly diverse, decentralised expressions of "unChristian" practice in Europe and America suggests otherwise. Once the spiritual authoritarianism of Christendom was declared to be in abeyance, people began to adopt a much wider spectrum of positions, covering territory theologians have not dared occupy for a thousand years. And this is not just to be expected; it is to be celebrated. It represents a gradual, and quite organic, restoration of state of affairs truly authentic to pre-Christianity—one that puts clear water between itself and Christendom, and thrives in its own right. By acknowledging the lesson taught by Asad and his fellow social constructionists—that "religion" is a term with a specific history and social context that limits its relevance—we are freed from the expectation to conform to the implicit standard of what "counts" as a religion. Rather than trying to revive ancient spiritualities by consciously trying to reconstruct specific rites and rituals, we have delivered a spiritual environment similar in key respects to that of the ancient world, without even meaning to. Though what Pagans think and do is thoroughly contemporary; the fact that we're all doing it differently, in ways concordant with our particular contexts, is quintessentially pre-Christian.

Like the common heritage that gave some semblance of unity to the Classical world in the face of the conquering army of Christ, so it is with Paganism today. As Ethan Doyle White points out, Pagans are united not by a common set of rituals, beliefs, or literary canon, but by a common social history; involving diverse groups exchanging ideas, practices, concerns, and themes over time, who began appearing in the 1800s, all drawing on the pre-Christian past in various ways[44]. Just as there are Dharmic religions (who look to Dharma), or Abrahamic religions (who look to Abraham and his legacy), so, Doyle White argues, there are Pagan ones (who look to the pre-Christian inhabitants of Europe). But this observation also points out a crucial difference between the Pagan religions of today, and the Abrahamic religions, especially Christianity; Abrahamic faiths tend to focus upon the teachings of a specific prophet—Jesus, Moses, Muham-

---

44 Doyle-White, E. (2012) **"In Defence of Pagan Studies: A Response to Davidsen's Critique"** in *The Pomegranate: The International Journal of Pagan Studies*, Vol. 14, No. 1, pp. 5-21.

mad—and earnestly affirm and search for compliance with such figures' singular authority. All other trusted teachers and texts are judged by their compliance with the truth stated by these great men; a truth which itself originally comes from a [singular] divine source. Paganisms, however, both past and present, look to many different sources of authority – without any one of these trumping the others.

BEYOND THE BIG TENT, AND INTO THE EARTHLY CITY

Although this epistemology is applied extensively in practice, the theory has yet to catch up. Many authors within the community and in the academy still attempt to define "Paganism" with reference to the everyday definition of "religion"—as a bounded belief system pertaining to spiritual matters. Rather than allowing for a historical understanding of contemporary and ancient pagan spiritualities—whose connections are constructed through the relationships between Pagans living and dead – it is assumed that the question "What is Paganism?" can be answered with reference to a particular set of ideas, that owe their validity to a single authoritative source. In doing this, we treat Christianity – with its emphasis on just such an arrangement - as the gold standard to which we must aspire. We see this clearly in attempts to create a "Big Tent" of Paganism, based as they are around a desire to establish certain broadly-worded statements of belief. Do you, like the Pagan Federation, believe in the role of the feminine in the godhead? Theological pluralism? Sacredness of nature? Perhaps Paganism is—as Margarian Bridger and Stephen Hergest argued, a triangle –with strong polytheism, an aspecting pantheism, and Jungian humanism at its points?[45] Or do we describe Paganism with reference to four poles—Nature, Deity, Community and the Self?[46] Such efforts are interesting, and noble— but they nonetheless attempt to shape Paganism after the fashion of the Christian *ecclesia*—a community joined by

common belief[s]—and as a result, fail to do justice to our traditions. Rather than devote our energies to dreaming into being successors to the older, pre-Christian relationships that were barely hinted at by the word *hellenismos*, we instead spend a lot of time and effort trying to herd conceptual cats.

But such efforts are doomed to either shoe-horning the wild variety of Pagan lived experience into a conceptual prison, or being so broad as to be empty of usefulness or rigour. We are left with Hobson's choice, of either leaving some Pagans out in the cold, or frogmarching those who would rather be outside the tent—often people of colour and indigenous communities—into its confines. Rather than create our own discourse about how our communities fit together, as Foucault might suggest we do[47], we consistently adopt the familiar mythos of the powerful.

The problem with a tent, is that it is a pre-defined space—it has a canopy, canvas walls, pegs, ropes, and—most of all—poles. All these things delimit the space, setting its dimensions firmly in time and place, rendering it static. If anybody tries to move any of these components, there is a very real risk the entire edifice will come crashing down.

Rather than create our own discourse about how our communities fit together, as Foucault might suggest we do, we consistently adopt the familiar mythos of the powerful.

Paganism, as a movement encompassing a range of very distinct religions, is ever-changing, ever-moving, ever-shifting. As such, it is as profoundly un-like a tent as you can imagine. Instead, Paganism is much more like a spontaneous gathering of people, in a place open to the elements—a crowd, a throng, a rally, a carnival. And as it has been going on for some time, it has become the permanent version of these: a city.

Cities do not have fixed borders, edges, limits in the same way that a tent does. Though we can easily point out the dimensions of a city in any given moment, this act is in no way is that definitive—indeed, cities are constantly changing in population and extent. All you need is for more people to come in, or for some others to leave, for some buildings to be built or torn down, and you have changed the city's limits. Nor is a city defined by single function or concept. Certainly, something will have attracted the first settlers there—a spring, a fertile field, a crossing place, or a defensible hill—but oftentimes this feature will vanish and be forgotten as the city grows. Over time, the city will gain its own character, based on the people

45   Bridger, M. and Hergest, S. (1997) *Pagan Deism: Three Views* in The *Pomegranate: The International Journal of Pagan Studies* Vol. 1 No. 1 pp. 37-42.

46   **Beckett, J. (2014) The Four Centers of Paganism** in *Under the Ancient Oaks (Patheos)*. Available at http://www.patheos.com/blogs/johnbeckett/2014/05/the-four-centers-of-paganism.html. Last accessed on 13/09/2015.

47   Foucault, M. (1972) *The Archaeology of Knowledge*, trans. A. M. Sheridan Smith. Routledge: London.

who have lived there, the land upon which it is built, and the events that have happened there. In short, what defines a city—and attracts more people to it—is not any one thing you find within it, but rather its history; the ongoing story of its making.

*Accordingly, two **cities** have been formed by two loves: **the earthly** by the love of self, even to the contempt of God; the heavenly by the love of God, even to the contempt of self. The former, in a word, glories in itself, the latter in the Lord.*[48]

Saint Augustine of Hippo once wrote a searing invective against what he called "The Earthly City" - a metaphor for the *disciplina* of the Roman Empire and all polytheistic societies. For Augustine, in such places it was Mankind who was the measure of all things, and not the Holy Spirit to which he professed allegiance. He exhorted Christendom to dwell instead within the City of God, wherein it was God, not mankind, who was the subject of devotion, and therefore the absolute standard against which society was weighed.

It is, perhaps, unfair of us to be too hard on Augustine. The Roman Empire was indeed an evil Empire; in which many bad men were raised up to a station they did not deserve. But Augustine's vision of the City of God and the Earthly City - one holy, one fallen, each centred on one thing - is, in the terms I have lain out above, less of a tale of two cities, but more of a tale of two big tents, with big poles in their middle. The reality behind Augustine's metaphor was, of course, but one city—Rome—that had yet to decide whether to accept the Divine Providence of Christ Crucified. In that choice, Augustine saw all of human history.

But in Augustine's Earthly City, we can see an echo of our own situation. His City of the Pagans did not recognise the total authority of the One True God, and neither do we. In echoing this refusal, we share in a key aspect of our ancestors' broader attitude toward the spiritual. But against Augustine, I would say that the true solution to the iniquity of Empire is not to choose an Emperor-God over a line of God-Emperors—but to dispense with the throne upon which both would sit. The Earthly City - if by that, we mean the example of Ancient Europe that inspires Pagans today, and not

the decadent late-Imperial Rome that Augus-tine knew - has no one king, no one centre, no one idol to occlude the vibrancy and variety on its streets. Let us not search in vain for the one public square, the one scenic landmark, the one ancient temple, the one leader who shall take precedence. Let us not worry unnecessarily over the matter of the gods; but explore it with curiosity, and accept the inevitably of many answers to the same questions. Let us leave belief-- and all the problematic baggage that it carries—behind. For there are far more important conversations; over how we should govern ourselves, about the security of our water and our weather, and about who our friends [and enemies] are. Because the more situated, the more contemporary, the more specific in time and space, the more rooted in the pragmatic concerns and the lived experiences of people today our spirituality is, the more like the wisdom of the ancients it becomes. Let us no longer falsely aspire to dwell in the City of God – obsessed with abstraction and unattainable discipline – but rather build together an *Earthy* city – where we are all sensitive to the way we need to live now, and are free to do so.

And may no one god, nor no one man, be the measure of all.•

> *The true solution to the iniquity of Empire is not to choose an Emperor-God over a line of God-Emperors—but to dispense with the throne upon which both would sit.*

Jonathan Woolley

is an animist druid from the rolling green hill country of Oxfordshire; part faun, part otter, totally gay. A leftist anthropologist by training, he spends his days talking with gods and men, reading Spinoza and Ostrom, and thinking up reasons why he deserves brownies. Jonathan maintains a blog about his academic fieldwork called BROAD PATHWAYS.

48   Augustine, Saint – Bishop of Hippo (2014) *De civitate Dei – English and Latin.* Harvard University Press: Cambridge MA.

Response To Amergin

(Chris Worlow)

I am the sparks between crossed blades
the gleam in the sky before dawn
I am the star flashing across the heavens
I am the wind among the trees

I am the runner in the forest
I am the song upon the breeze
I am the light in your eyes

as you awaken

I am the glint of steel in firelight

I am the bird taking flight on the breeze
I am the fire in the forge
I am the river that you cross
I am the time between two days

I am the darkness as you blink
I am the pen set down

upon the table
I am the tiger glancing forward

I am the phoenix's ashes on the pyre

I am the flame seen from far away

I am the scent half-caught in the air

I am the hidden waiting to be found

I am the chalice raised

full and high

I am the storm unfurling wide
the color half-remembered
I am the poem half-forgotten

the lyre just restrung

I am thoughts unbidden
I am passion half-forgotten
I am the gaze half-seen

I am inertia

I am the raven within its egg
I am the shadow cast by the earth
I am the tower without doors
the sky without horizon

Chris Worlow

Chris Worlow's love of poetry began with John Keats and poems about beautiful faerie women without mercy. Since then, Chris has used poetry to various spiritual and aesthetic ends, leading into eclecticism of all kinds. And faeries. Lots of faeries. As a grad student, Chris studied Shakespeare, earning a doctorate while writing a dissertation on finding models for positive political action and participation in Shakespeare's plays. Chris sees the purposes of life, art, and magic as including the discovery and creation of meaning and significance.

No Hope, No Despair

Towards a polytheist nihilism (Lo)

The world is increasingly unthinkable—a world of planetary disasters, emerging pandemics, tectonic shifts, strange weather, oil-drenched seascapes, and the furtive, always-looming threat of extinction. In spite of our daily concerns, wants, and desires, it is increasingly difficult to comprehend the world in which we live and of which we are a part. To confront this idea is to confront an absolute limit to our ability to adequately understand the world at all.

- Eugene Thacker, *In the Dust of this Planet*

BAPTISM IN THE RUBICON

What is initiation? It can be many things: a jail cell; a birthday party; a diagnosis; a drug trip; a first child; joy; loss. But it is also only one thing: the acknowledgment of that which was previously unknown or simply dismissed. The moment when an unbearable pain becomes bearable.

For those of us who were not raised by socialist families, coming into our own as anti-capitalists was a process of initiation, especially if some of us happened to come upon Rand or Rothbard first. The environmental movement and radical green movements have been undergoing an initiation lately as well, of the likes that hasn't been seen since its inception in response to the beginning of the atomic age: the world's initiation into adulthood (an adulthood we have squandered). We are being faced with the realization that solar panels and Priuses are not enough to cure the world. The terrible conjuration before us appears in hues of brown and gray, and it spreads. As the anonymous author of *Desert*, a treatise on eco-anarchist despair, writes: "something haunts [us]". Environmentalists and leftist radicals the world over are beginning to see that the project of humanism is built on the backs of restless dead as they peer through the hagstone.

The ritual is slow and vast, but many radicals still resist the incantations and symbols of collapse despite the fact that they are themselves moving in time with the drum and chant. But all it takes is a look to the countless outpouring of scientific articles to begin to understand that the writing is on the wall. The Earth is due to warm 0.1 degree Celcius over the course of 2015[49]. Our oceans continue to acidify[50]. Prolonged drought conditions all over the world hinder forests' ability to grow[51] and sequester carbon. Permafrost is melting, releasing even more ancient CO_2 into the atmosphere. Sea levels are rising as ice melts, and the clock is ticking for low-lying nations like Bangladesh, and parts of other countries like India and China will face mass displacements of millions in the coming decades. Tens of thousands will die every year as catastrophic weather events continue to grow in power and frequency.

And that's to not even touch on the mass extinction event already silently disappearing dozens if not hundreds of plant and animal species[52] every day, like a ghostly gestapo carrying out the machinations of a chthonic dictator.

Thylacinus cynocephalus.

Pinguinus impennis.

Incilius periglenes.

These are now but epithets for the Anthropocene. Know them, use them. There will be many more to come.

SELF-WORSHIP IN THE CHURCH OF PROGRESS

In *Straw Dogs*, John Gray argues that humanism is the mass opiate of our time; though credited to Socrates, who himself said that he oftentimes did the bidding of his *daimon*, humanism's iron grip and obsession with salvation by (any) another name is more a holdover from pre-Enlightenment Christianity than anything else:

49   .https://www.newscientist.com/article/mg22730324-200-earth-now-
       halfway-to-un-global-warming-limit/

50   .http://phys.org/news/2014-10-scientists-alarm-ocean-
       acidification.html

51   http://phys.org/news/2015-07-drought-impact-forests.html

52   http://www.huffingtonpost.com/2010/08/17/un-environment-
       programme-_n_684562.html

"In monotheistic faiths God is the final guarantee of meaning in human life. For [the Earth-System of the Gaia Hypothesis], human life has no more meaning than the life of slime mould."[53]

Here, he means what he says, but in this he also means for the monotheistic—specifically Christian—God to be synonymous with science and progress. We are uplifted in similar ways by the both of them in their promises of immortality, of homogeneity and purity, of an end to suffering, of meaning made for us. Promissory materialism is not unlike fundamentalist belief in the second coming of the messiah; both take for granted the unsubstantiated belief that a future event will legitimize the superstition and sort out all of the unanswered questions once and for all. *Worry not.*

Progress, though, is a myth. Its believers are in a never-ending war against the reality that humans are no better, no smarter, and no more masters of their destiny than any other animal on the earth. That which sets us apart is simply that we have the capacity to know that we are animal... and perhaps more importantly, the capacity to deny it. Calling on Schopenhauer, Gray writes:

"Our intellects are not impartial observers of the world but active participants in it. They shape a view of it that helps us in our struggles. Among the imaginary constructions created by the intellect working in the service of the will, perhaps the most delusive is the view it gives us of ourselves – as continuing, unified individuals."[54]

It is not God that is dead. In fact, on the contrary: it is *we* that are dead!

ANIMISM IS HERE

Refutation of progress and scientistic materialism tends to leave us with a sinking in our hearts. If pursuing higher and higher orders of technological complexity, or cybernetic immortality, or some kind of materialist truth are lies not worth putting our faith into, then what is? Human existence could then be said to be comprised of nothing more than an intricate tapestry of richly interwoven delusions, each of them just as far from the truth as the next. Moreover, what is truth, then? Is there anything beyond that which our evolutionary history, driven by little more than random mutation,

deems important for our survival? Is there some kind of truth that our animal cousins cannot know? Some secret we can share amongst ourselves?

These, I'm afraid, are the wrong questions.

Truth is experiential. It is not the thoughts that pass through the mind of a contemplative student of existence, it is the life that begins to be lived once a revelation is reached. It is not that which makes you unafraid of death, it is *being* unafraid of death. It is not thinking, it is doing. It is here, on earth, or there, in the otherworlds.

Words and actions are meant to be manifest, not hoarded like currency in anticipation of investment.

Animism is here, though. It is the primal religion common to all of us, and yes, the animals too. It is the fundamental recognition that what is central to our being lies outside of us and--most times-- outside of our control. In this, right action and right relationship are one and the same. Other peoples, and the occasional rare westerner, who have resisted the myth of humanism and progress know this.

Grow flowers; mend clothes; cook meals; sacrifice in exchange for the sacrifice that makes your life possible. Nature is a gift economy where the gifts of survival are given freely and taken freely. These are some of the truths.

And the world is full of Gods – that is another.

> ## *Progress, though, is a myth. Its believers are in a never-ending war against the reality that humans are no better, no smarter, and no more masters of their destiny than any other animal on the earth.*

DELUDED GODS

It may be argued that gods of technology are lying to Themselves for having bought into the myth of our exceptionalism. But They are not infallible – we know this. Should the industrial world collapse, will these holy proponents of industry struggle to find a reason to live like some of us likely will? I would not be surprised; but then parts of Them might already be dying every day a worker throws themselves off a factory building in Shenzhen or hangs themselves in Aokigahara. Their tears are the shoes of bridge jumpers that wash to shore. What would a follower do if their God committed suicide?

We know many, if not all, of the Gods are immortal, not invincible, and wise but not all-knowing. Do They have free will? Do They have the capacity to tell lies because They Themselves believe them? I don't think this matters beyond

---

53   John Gray, Straw Dogs (NEED PAGE)
54   John Gray, Straw Dogs (NEED PAGE)

proving that we would not be alone in our propensity for self-deception. Another nail in the coffin for human uniqueness. But just as likely this is not the case. Their evolution might not have ever had a use for fantasy and delusion in the way that ours does. There's a reason that the gods are said to be far-seeing.

I don't know about you, but I don't worship the Gods because they are better than me. Wiser, stronger, older, more powerful, maybe, but not better. The Gods, too, are slime mould to the universe. Don't let Their aspirations for power and glory, or the vastness of their accomplishments fool you. I worship them because there is something in Them that I choose to acknowledge in a way we can both agree on. It isn't even about belief – it's simply a matter of voluntary association.

SACRED GRIEVING

We are all grieving, for with existence comes loss. Even the Gods weep for lost comrades, children, lovers. We honor Their losses; for some of us, this is an annual affair. For others, there is always a place for it on Their shrine. But our understanding is limited to mythic grief; few, I imagine, if any, can say that they have felt the full force of a Holy Power's despair, here and now, instead of feeling simply the reverberations of a tragedy that happened—or perhaps continues to happen—beyond our scope of time and space.

Children, after all, learn to navigate the world of emotions from their parents. If they are shielded from tragedy and sadness, then they might struggle with experiencing or conveying them later.

I sense that our humanist delusions have soured our insides and constipated us. There are many things we cannot stomach in their purest form, and require dilution. There are other things that, when consumed, masticated, absorbed, have trouble being released out of the bowels and back into the world of the living. The circle continues to break down in a number of ways.

The longer we hold onto the remnants of this Food, the more likely it is to grow septic within us.

If you have tears, let them fall. If you have rage, let it burn.

Allow yourself to weep with the Gods, for they know as well as we do what the next century will bring. Like us they marvel in horror at our capacity to raze our only home, salt our only field, soil our only bed.

If you have tears, let them fall. If you have rage, let it burn.

We are now become the child who happens upon their parents' imperfections. They can hurt, they can cry, they can make the most terrific mistakes; oh, how they bleed like us also! We can either accept this and gently bring them down from the pedestal, or we can nurse our horror at the obscenity of their limitations.

NIHILISM NOW, APOCALYPSE LATER

Yamaoka Tesshu, as a young student of Zen, visited one master after another. He called upon Dokuon of Shokoku.

Desiring to show his attainment, he said: "The mind, Buddha, and sentient beings, after all, do not exist. The true nature of phenomena is emptiness. There is no realization, no delusion, no sage, no mediocrity. There is no giving and nothing to be received."

Dokuon, who was smoking quietly, said nothing. Suddenly he whacked Yamaoka with his bamboo pipe. This made the youth quite angry.

"If nothing exists," inquired Dokuon, "where did this anger come from?"

– Zen Koan[55]

Nihilism has a very poor reputation, misappropriated in similar ways to the term "anarchy". It doesn't have an image problem, because to recognize the importance of image is to negate what nihilism is. It cannot be sold, bought, or made appealing by the hegemonic standards of humanist values.

Because it is, at its core, a profound acceptance. It accepts —no, *embraces*—the assertion that we are all of equal meaning and equal value in the face of nature, and therefore, too, the face of death. Humanism by its very nature cannot accept these things. It rejects the temporality of existence, the inevitability of old age and death. To a humanist, we have the ability to all someday be elevated to a transcendental godhood sustained by self-worship and presently unfathomable technology.

But the humanist project was doomed from the start. While some fantasize about colonizing space or uploading our brains into computers (never asking, of course, *whose* computers), it is, in reality, constantly teetering on the brink of absurdism. The risk of paradox is always too close for comfort.

It seems to me that naturalists, which those of us who truly believe in the Gods and who recognize our inherent propensity for animism really are, don't suffer from existential

---

55 .http://www.ashidakim.com/zenkoans/82nothingexists.html

threats like these. Or at least, not in the same way or to the same degree. It is no coincidence that those obsessed with higher orders and inherent purpose should be consumed with cheating death and afraid of their own reflection.

We should not be afraid at the prospect of making our own meaning.

But all things must someday come to an end. Whether us, our Gods, or our civilizations, acceptance need not change our relationship to the spirits of Holy Powers, just as a terminal illness need not change our relationship to friends and loved ones. In fact, it can even have the opposite effect: solidarity flourishes.

MAKING MEANING

We should embrace the possibilities that polytheist nihilism can unearth for us. But we cannot do that without first learning to recognize what we have lost, what we are *currently* losing, and accepting them as things that we, whether as individuals or movements, could not change. Nihilism as acceptance is not achievable without the initiation of mourning. Without it, it is just another stage of grief in the guise of hedonism, or worse: simple, vulgar, pessimism.

We should not be afraid at the prospect of making our own meaning. For many of us, our Gods are said to have done this themselves in our many accounts of creation—we should look to these examples of self-made meaning and be inspired at how wondrous the result can be. If not, we run the risk of falling into despair, which is counter-productive to the project of re-integration with the earth on its own terms. To not turn back, regardless if it's too late, is to embrace absurdism and to condemn all living things to the fate we've left for them. Is it not better to embrace the dying man than to ignore him laying in the street? It is nihilism's business to condemn only that which, being weighed and measured, is found useless to the truth of here and now. And as the author of one of the more prominent explanations of gender nihilism posits, these sorts of projects should aim to be just that: projects. If we are honest with ourselves, these better serve to "[designate] a horizon rather than an actuality"[56]. A wide horizon indeed.

This is not to say that we should abandon culture to the trenches—primitivist exasperation and insurrectionary anger inevitably become seductive when contemplating nihilism, this is true. But it is also ironic that the primitivists, with all their talk of a pristine, ahistorical, human state, sow the seeds of their own irrelevance: it is the power of the symbol that allowed our distant ancestors to bring forth the first inanimate tool from the realm of abstraction. It is that which allows us to communicate with the otherworld and each other. After all, isn't the language of the modern human little different from the taunts of the jaybird or the chemical chatter of a redwood community? To reject that which makes us human, whether by primitivist or transhumanist philosophy, once again ignores our precarious place here in favor of escapism and mere aesthetics.

Abandon the illusion of self-determination. Refocus on that which *is* within our sphere of influence. That sphere may seem fearfully small compared to what the humanist, capitalist, scientist overculture has promised, and it is. But the places that are left are our real seats of power. Learn a skill. Explore the mysteries of autosacrifice. Manifest abstraction. Blood, sweat, and tears *are potent*. (This is a cliché, but those who avoid them only have something to sell.)

Our importance in the world may not be real. The Gods may not be real. *We* may not be real[57]. But I say They—and we—are more than real enough. Now is time to realize that the unbearable may in fact be just the opposite.

A gift is coming to you, even as the days become numbered.

Do you have one ready to give in return?

Lo

is an anti-humanist polytheist, and a graphic novel writer/artist. They blog at rotwork.wordpress.com & currently reside about Cascadia, though mostly in Vancouver.

---

56 https://automaticwriting1.wordpress.com/2015/02/12/gender-nihilism/

57 http://www.technologyreview.com/view/429561/the-measurement-that-would-reveal-the-universe-as-a-computer-simulation/

Are The Gods On Our Side?
(Heathen Chinese)

The writers in this journal have a shared agenda: the end of capitalism. It's tempting to declare definitively that the gods are anti-capitalist as well, but relationships between deities and their individual and collective worshipers are more complicated than that. If one accepts the premise that the gods are powers autonomous from humans, then they necessarily have their own agendas, which may or may not coincide with ours.

In acknowledging the individuality and diversity of gods and spirits, it becomes difficult to make broad generalizations. However, at a more localized level, some generalized characteristics can still be said to be inherent within the "function" of specific kinds of spirits. Spirits which dwell in trees typically do not like those trees being cut down. Note that this does not necessarily mean that a specific spirit dwelling in a specific tree is against *any* tree being cut down, though some might very well feel that way given the terrifying rate of deforestation these days. However, it's fairly certain that a spirit will object to its *own* home being destroyed.

Ancestral spirits, at least from a Chinese worldview, generally want their descendants' behavior to reflect honorably upon their names and are predisposed to favor their descendants' material survival, which is a prerequisite for the continuation of the family lineage. "Hungry ghosts," or the restless dead, are by definition inclined to draw attention to themselves and their deaths in some manner or another.

All of these classes of spirits have agendas which may very well coincide with anti-capitalist struggles against the destruction of ecosystems, the killing of youths of certain ancestral lineages, etc. Their assistance in these struggles should be sought out, when appropriate.

But what of the gods, whose agendas are both vaster and more varied than those of local spirits and the spirits of the dead? Where do they stand in the struggles of their worshipers?

GODS AND THEIR WORSHIPERS

In the "Strong Roots and Wide Branches: Essentials of Polytheism" presentation at Pantheacon 2015, River Devora and Anomalous Thracian suggested a working definition of gods: gods are distinguished from other beings with similar degrees of power over mortal lives by having oaths, obligations, agreements or some other form of ongoing give-and-take relationship with group(s) of said mortals. Thus, one may make the generalization that the gods are interested in upholding agreements and maintaining relationships with humans who make an effort to do the same.

So what happens when, humans being humans, conflict arises within or between those groups? If one group or subgroup has broken the "terms" of their agreement with the god through dishonorable conduct or impiety, then the god may show favor to one side over the other, perhaps by granting victory in a decisive battle. However, as occurs much more frequently, conflicts such as class struggle remain embedded within society over longer periods of time.

GUAN DI

One of the primary gods that I worship, Guan Di, provides an interesting case study here. As was mentioned in Ned Levin's 2014 article "Hong Kong Protests: Guan Yu is the People's Deity," Guan Di is worshiped by cops, gangsters and protestors alike in Hong Kong. When a society falls apart or explodes due to its internal contradictions, how does a god like Guan Di deal with those conflicts between his various worshipers?

Being a mortal, I cannot answer for Guan Di. However, Prasenjit Duara's 1988 article "Superscribing Symbols: The Myth of Guandi, Chinese God of War," published in *The Journal of Asian Studies*, has shown that these types of contradictions are nothing new for Guan Di.

Before his apotheosis, the man named Guan Yu was a mortal warrior and general in the late Han Dynasty (he died in 220 CE) who participated in the suppression of a Daoist-influenced millenarian movement known as the Yellow Turban Rebellion and fought in the civil wars that ensued. Centuries after his death, both Buddhists and Daoists claimed Guan Yu as a protector figure within their respective pantheons.

In 1615, the Ming imperial government granted him the title "Di," which means "Emperor". However, there was also a massive expansion of his popular worship outside of Buddhist, Daoist *and* imperial religious organizations during the same time period.

Duara cites the research of Huang Huajie, which situates the spread of the popularity of Guan Di within a historical context in which "the rural economy became increasingly commercialized" and traditional forms of social organization were weakened:

> Huang Huajie links Guan Yu's growing popularity in the Ming (1368-1644) and the Qing (1644-1911) to the great socioeconomic changes of the era, which of course also enabled the popular media to spread. As the rural economy became increasingly commercialized, self-sufficient kin-based communities tended to disintegrate. In their place, settlements came to be composed of unrelated kin groups, merchants for whom sojourning had become a way of life, and marginal peoples without a community, such as vagrants and bandits.[58]

In other words, Guan Di's popularity does not exist in *spite* of class struggle but *because* of it. Duara writes that "for the rootless bandits and rebels of secret societies, the oath of loyalty that Guan Yu upheld gained an unparalleled salience"[59] and that "for them, the oath symbolized loyalty to brother-

---

58: Duara, Prasenjit. "Superscribing Symbols: The Myth of Guandi, Chinese God of War." *The Journal of Asian Studies* 47.4 (1988): 781-2
59: p. 782

hood, not to the state that had been their enemy"[60]. Ironically, many of the secret societies devoted to the overthrow of the Qing Dynasty subsequently formed the nucleus of the gangs (Triads) referenced in Levin's article, some of which have been accused of attacking protestors on behalf of the police—contradictions upon contradictions. There's also an urban legend that Guan Di statues in Triad shrines hold the *guan dao* (Guan Di's distinctive polearm) in the left hand, whereas Guan Di statues in the shrines of policemen and ordinary citizens hold the *guan dao* in the right hand.

Duara asks, "If a myth represents radically discontinuous meanings, if its symbols are pursued by particular groups only for their own particular purposes, how can it continue to impart legitimacy so widely across the culture?"[61]. She proposes a theory that she calls "the superscription of symbols." She contrasts "superscription" to "erasure," writing that "the very mechanism of superscription necessarily requires the preservation of at least some of the other voices that surround the symbol,"[62] rather than the total obliteration of those voices.

Thus, two diametrically opposed views of Guan Di (i.e. champion of the imperial dynasty vs. divine witness to the initiation oaths of secret societies trying to overthrow said dynasty) are linked to one another through their relationship to a common predecessor (i.e., the earliest Buddhist and/or Daoist conceptions of Guan Yu as a paragon of loyalty and protector of the faithful).

Finally, Guan Di also provides an example of a god intervening on only one side of a conflict: he was one of the gods who possessed insurgents during the anti-foreign and anti-Christian Boxer Rebellion of 1900. He was also credited with defeating a proposed law that would have forced the Chinese in Santa Cruz, California to move outside of city limits, as historian Sandy Lydon relates in *Chinese Gold*[63].

IMPLICATIONS

It seems reasonable to conclude that Guan Di has, at times, answered the prayers of both sides of a conflict simultaneously. It seems further reasonable to extend this pattern to the ongoing conflict that some call "the class war." Guan Di has thousands and thousands of worshipers with whom he maintains relationship on both sides of said war.

60: p. 783

61: p. 779

62: p. 791

63: Lydon, Sandy. *Chinese Gold: The Chinese in the Monterey Bay Region.* Capitola: Capitola Book Co, 1985. (p. 280)

The gods of (primarily European) reconstructed polytheisms and neo-paganisms have fewer total worshipers in the world today than Guan Di does. However, this fact opens the possibility that individual worshipers' prayers and petitions will proportionally represent a larger "percentage" of a given deity's relationships and obligations. As the worship of many gods is restored in the West, it is therefore the *responsibility and duty* of anti-capitalist/anti-racist polytheists and neo-pagans to make their voices heard as loudly as possible. Ask for your gods' help in our collective struggles before the other side does.

That said, relationships to deities are not numbers games, and they're not majority-rule democracies. Guan Di is called "Emperor" for a reason – not because he is always aligned with temporal State power (obviously, he is not), but because he exercises sovereignty over the areas of life that he rules. Reciprocity is not a mechanical process with guaranteed quantifiable results, but an organic process founded upon autonomous choices and decisions by both parties – in other words, voluntary association.

CONCLUSION

It's tempting to declare that "the gods are anti-capitalist." With careful consideration of the case study of Guan Di, worshiped by cops and protesters alike, it would perhaps be more accurate to declare that "*our* gods are anti-capitalist," by which we would mean the specific gods that we are in relationship with. They are anti-capitalist not because it is innate in their nature but because they maintain relationships with us and answer our prayers, and because we in our turn make an effort to maintain relationship with *them* as we struggle daily against the impositions of Capital. We could all certainly use as much divine protection, aid and blessings as possible. It is not so much a question of whether the gods are *on* our side, but whether or not they are *at* our sides.•

HeathenChinese
is the son of Chinese immigrants. He is a diasporic Chinese polytheist living in the San Francisco Bay Area (stolen Ohlone land). He practices ancestor veneration and worships (among others) the warrior god Guan Di, who has had a presence in California since the mid-1800s. He writes sporadically at heathenchinese.wordpress.com.

Earth Goddesses Uprising
(P. Sufenas Virius Lupus)

Since the first Many Gods West conference—an historic and unprecedented gathering of polytheists from many traditions for rituals and presentations on diverse topics in Olympia, Washington, U.S.A.—in late July/early August of 2015, I've seen two blog posts—one by Finnchuill,[64] and one by Rhyd Wildermuth[65]—which have (amongst other things) discussed a variety of eschatological feeling that seems to be in the air at present.

I had a very good conversation at Many Gods West with Heathen Chinese on the first day of it at dinner which also ended up being eschatological. His presentation the following day was on Chinese millenarian movements, and was one of the most informative parts of the conference for me–I had heard of the Boxer Rebellion (late 19th/early 20th centuries CE) and the Yellow Turban Rebellion (late 2nd/early 3rd centuries CE),[66] but not the other movements he had discussed. I had not previously heard of the mystical and millenarian undercurrents of those movements that I had known about (outside of Heathen Chinese's own post on the Boxers), nor was I familiar with them in such great detail as given on that occasion.

In our conversation that Friday at dinner, he made passing mention of these movements, and commented on an interesting point of connection between the two of our spiritual practices and those of the movements in question: often the principal Divine Beings to whom people have been devoted in those empire-toppling situations, and certainly in his and my practices, have not been ancient and traditional, aeon-spanning Deities, but instead divinized or deified humans of various sorts. This not only intrigued me, it made me sit up even more attentively, and propelled what I spoke of next, which I will try to elaborate upon in what follows.

---

64 https://finnchuillsmast.wordpress.com/2015/08/16/the-wind-is-rising/

65 http://paganarch.com/2015/08/16/dahut-at-the-floodgate/

66 See Heathen Chinese's posts on these at http://godsandradicals.org/2015/06/03/uncontrolled-the-boxer-rebellion-of-1898-1900/ and
https://heathenchinese.wordpress.com/2013/04/01/millenarianism-pt-2-the-yellow-turbans/

I have previously written about the repeated frustrations of attempts at Greek eschatology (or, at least, regime change) in the current generation of Deities who are supreme in the Greek pantheon. Indeed, there may be something to be gained in looking at those patterns, and seeing where the next stage in that progression might come from, by looking at the impetus for each of the major regime changes that has occurred previously.

Readers may have a hint of this in the title of the present discussion. I have deliberately parodied the book *Earth God Rising*[67] with that title, because it was one of the first "properly pagan" (not Arthurian or Celtic) books I obtained and read in 1994 when I was in New York for college. For a thousand reasons, the book was not, in my opinion (then or now) very good, even though my critical skills were nowhere near

as sharp as they are now.[68] *My polytheist and revolutionary revisioning of the title is, I hope, an improvement, and a fair summary of what will follow.*

We have come, not only as polytheists and pagans but as a wider overculture, to think of "Mother Earth" as a kindly and all-embracing parent, Who it is implied to an extent is infinitely compassionate, always forgiving, and forever non-judgmental of Her erring and disrespectful children. The "Gaia hypothesis" that is much favored by many environmentalists, as well as scientifically-minded pagans as a theology as well as an ecological metaphor, often then gets combined in with this picture of Mother Earth as providing a place and nurturance to all of Her children equally. What has become apparent via the realities of climate change, how-

---

67   Alan Richardson, *Earth God Rising: The Return of the Male Mysteries* (St. Paul, MN: Llewellyn Publications, 1990).

68   The attempted universalizing of binary gendered mysteries implied in the title, and carried out in the course of the work, is only the start of how flawed and problematic the book seems to me more than twenty years since I read it!

ever, is that the natural cycles on Earth are entirely indifferent to human existence, despite being deeply impacted by our species' collective actions and the by-products of our current lifestyles and consumption patterns. The likelihood that any number of factors—from water scarcity to rising ocean levels, deforestation and increased temperatures, and a grand variety of related phenomena—may begin to cause massive die-offs in the human population in the coming century is all the more certain now, which makes eschatological thinking in terms of religious practice almost a necessity rather than the not-very-fun afterthought which some pagans have considered it for decades in their "this-world"-focused theological and practical viewpoints. Interestingly enough, this ferocity of Mother Nature and Mother Earth is prefigured in Greek myth perfectly with Gaia herself.

In Hesiod's *Theogony*, various primordial beings born out of Chaos begin to populate the cosmos, and after Gaia gives birth to several such beings parthenogenically (including Ouranos), she then begins to have offspring with Ouranos, including the Titans, the three elder Cyclopes, and the three Hekatoncheires ("hundred-handed"). Ouranos, however, finds the latter six offspring ugly and unsightly, and locks them deep within Gaia herself, not allowing them to come forth. This angers Gaia, and she produces iron and the sickle made from it, which she presents to her children with the words:

> "Yours is a reckless father; obey me, if you will,
> that we may punish your father's outrageous deed,
> for he was first to plot shameful actions."[69]

It is to be noted that Gaia's words seem to indicate that She would have been far more even-tempered had Her husband been more respectful and nurturing of his unusually-bodied children.[70] It is Her youngest Titanic son, Kronos, who takes

The likelihood that any number of factors—from water scarcity to rising ocean levels, deforestation and increased temperatures, and a grand variety of related phenomena—may begin to cause massive die-offs in the human population in the coming century is all the more certain now, which makes eschatological thinking in terms of religious practice almost a necessity

up the sickle and castrates His father, which ends up creating other Divine Beings (like Aphrodite) and Divine Races (like the Gigantes, on whom more later).

One would think that the Titans would have taken this message on board, and would have thus lead virtuous and exceptional lives themselves and in relation to their future offspring. It is not long in coming, however, before the ascendant Kronos Himself transgresses in a similar fashion, and begins eating His children after they are born, in fear that they might overthrow Him as well. At last, it is His wife Rhea, the Titanic generation's Earth Goddess, who likewise lays the plans for how to turn the tables on Her offending husband. She asks for the assistance of Gaia and Ouranos, and is taken to Crete to give birth to Zeus, Who forces His father to vomit up His siblings. With the assistance of the elder Cyclopes, He is given the thunderbolt and uses it to complete His divine coup and the bringing about of the world in the situation with which we are now familiar, with Zeus reigning supreme over the other Olympian Deities–His siblings, as well as some of His children.[71]

However, despite a number of prophecies that predict the overthrow of Zeus by future offspring, or an actual attempt at a coup with several Deities (Hera, Athena, and Poseidon),[72] Zeus continues to reign supreme over all the other Deities. The third Divine generation seems to be maintaining its order, for good and ill, and yet the third of the generations of Earth Goddesses—namely Demeter—is not without Her own complaints against Zeus, Who fathered Persephone on Her, and then married their daughter off without Demeter's permission to Her uncle Hades. In the *Homeric Hymn to Demeter*, in the narration of Her sadness at Her daughter's taking, Demeter wanders, comes to Eleusis, and through various circumstances attempts but fails to immortalize Demophoön. It is in another bout of sadness at Her double loss that she then brings about

---

69 Hesiod, *Theogony, Works and Days, Shield*, trans. Apostolos N. Athanassakis (Baltimore and London: The Johns Hopkins University Press, 1983), p. 17.

70 So much can be understood metaphorically in this for our modern situation, from the oppression of marginalized peoples—racially, disabled, and otherwise—to the threatened existences of so many other non-human species on our planet, which might stir the anger of Gaia against humans...or, in fact, all signs indicate it already has begun to

occur.

71 Hesiod, pp. 24-26.

72 For more on these, see the following blog post: https://aediculaantinoi.wordpress.com/2014/07/26/the-lack-of-greek-eschatology/ .

the famine that threatens not only human and other animal life due to the non-productivity of the Earth, but also the offerings given to the Deities, whereupon they are forced to seek terms with Her. It is Her mother, the Earth Goddess Rhea, Who is the crucial negotiatrix in this settlement with Demeter which returns Persephone to her for part of the year, and likewise results in the founding of the Eleusinian Mysteries.

While an etiology of the annual seasonal shifts, and of the origins of Spring and Winter in particular, is often read into this earliest version of the story of Demeter and Persephone, the text of the Homeric Hymn itself doesn't suggest that at all, and it is later writers who explicitly take up that theme. What I find most interesting about this text is something discussed in brief by a number of scholars, including Jenny Strauss Clay, Helene Foley, and Sarah Iles Johnston,[73] which is that the Eleusinian Mysteries might be a second-rate replacement for the failed immortalization of Demophoön. While this may not seem as earth-shattering as it is in actuality, it then prompts the question of why Demeter was interested in Demophoön's immortalization in the first place, if not simply and only as a surrogate for Her lost daughter. What these scholars suggest, and what I entirely agree with, is that it was Demeter's intention to bring about a challenge to Zeus' rule by the newly-immortalized Demophoön. That effort having failed, however (and this is my own interpretation of the matter), it is now up to the humans who have undergone the Eleusinian Mysteries—who have earned a special place in the Greek afterlife outside of the moldering forgetfulness of the shades in Hades nor the possibility of reincarnation–to form Demeter's new army held in reserve that may, in turn, bring about the overthrow of Zeus' rule on Olympus. As ever, thus, the Earth Goddess in each generation of Greek Divine regimes is the source of the uprising which brings about the subsequent order and shapes the future era.

> *Capitalism's excesses have collapsed "Works and Days" into a singular juggernaut that would make Hesiod—and I'd venture to say does make all of the Deities—groan with dismay and cry out with Their devotees for justice and peace.*

This puts the importance of those divine practices—including initiation in Mystery traditions—and the possibility of human apotheosis at an entirely different and more significant level of immediacy and importance than it might otherwise be in one's view of the ancient Greek Deities, the span of Hellenic cosmic ages, and their implications for both personal, terrestrial, and cosmic eschatology. Given that the talk that Heathen Chinese and myself had on these subjects was in Olympia, perhaps it was especially appropriate that the subjects turned to the ultimate questions of who reigns in Olympus, and how such determinations are made: ever and always at the discretion of the Earth Goddesses.

Myth does not literally reflect what Deities do, think, or are like of necessity, despite mythic narratives being their own kind of revelatory insight into the nature of particular Deities and their relationships with one another, the cosmos, and with humans. What always comes through in tellings of myths–in the modern world as equally as in the ancient world–is that Deities and their functions are analogized, whether deliberately or not, to the human legal and social world, its particularities, its shape and expected order of operations. The Greeks, and the Romans after them, could not conceive of a culture in stature or eminence beyond their own, with its laws and institutions exemplifying a small island of perfection amidst a seething morass of barbarians at every border. It is thus probably no surprise that they did not see fit to engage in mythic narrative conceptions of the end of their own age via discussing the end of the current era of Deities. Every attempt at such Divine reorganization is thwarted by the ever-insightful and prescient Zeus, sometimes with the assistance of Divine Beings from the previous generation, like Thetis who prevented the coup of Hera, Athena, and Poseidon.[74] Thus, we have no narrative like the Germanic Ragnarok, nor the Hindu conception of the Four Ages; each of those cultures, when they recorded those

---

73   See the much more in-depth discussion of this matter, and the work of these (and other) scholars on it, which I've done previously in P. Sufenas Virius Lupus, "Demeter's Other Children: Demophoön and the Eleusinian Mysteries," in Melitta Benu and Rebecca Buchanan (eds)., *Potnia: A Devotional Anthology in Honor of Demeter* (Asheville, NC: Bibliotheca Alexandrina, 2014), pp. 190-198.

74   On this coup, see the only ancient source that mentions it (Homer's *Iliad*): A. T. Murray (ed./trans), *Homer, Iliad*, revised by Murray F. Wyatt, 2 volumes (Cambridge: Harvard University Press, 1999), Vol. 1, pp. 42-43 (Book 1 lines 396-406); Vol. 2, pp. 86-87 (Book 14 lines 271-279). . Given that this is the case, will any future uprisings then feature not only perhaps the Titans, but likewise their other wronged siblings, the Hekatoncheires? One can only speculate.

myths, had been through regime changes on a societal level that were profound, on several occasions in semi-recorded or orally transmitted history. For the Greeks and the Romans after them, the regime change with the eventual hegemony of Christianity occurred before it could be anticipated, and the myths of the pre-Christian period were soon subverted to support the ascendant Christian cosmology. The Christian deities were like Zeus only more moral, more powerful, and without birth (with one exception, of course!).

The one possible exception to this trend might be via the contested figure of Claudian, a late antique Latin poet from Alexandria who lived in the later fourth and early fifth centuries CE, who wrote of polytheistic themes but had Christian patrons in the general Stilicho and the Emperor Honorius. Given that he straddled the crux of the Roman Empire's turn from polytheism to hegemonic Nicene Christianity, perhaps we can see in the truncated text of one of his shorter poems, the *Gigantomachia*, a hearkening back to some of the themes mentioned previously as understood in his precarious age. Though the tradition of the "Gigantomachy" was long-standing, possibly dating back to Homer and certainly Hesiod's age (both of whom allude to later episodes and associations with it), great variations in its text and interpretation existed, and the figures upon whom it focused or incorporated into its tradition (e.g. the Titans, Typhon, the Aloadae, etc.) varied greatly. However, the Olympian generation of Deities tended to be featured—especially Athena—and likewise the assistance of Herakles (a half-mortal son of Zeus) was often thought necessary in the winning of the battle which involved the uprising of the Gigantes (often understood as "Giants," though they are not portrayed as of unusual size, but sometimes are given serpentine legs and humanoid bodies) against the reigning Olympians or Titans. In Claudian's version, the impetus for the revolt of the Gigantes is once again Gaia, their mother, who is angry at the Olympians for their oppressive imprisonment of the Titans.

"Children, ye shall conquer heaven: all that ye see is the prize of victory; win, and the universe is yours. At last shall Saturn's son feel the weight of my wrath; shall recognize Earth's power. What! can any force conquer me? Has Cybele born sons superior to mine? Why has Earth no honour? Why is she ever condemned to bitter loss? Has any form of injury passed me by? There hangs luckless Prometheus in yon Scythian vale, feeding the

vulture on his living breast; yonder, Atlas supports the weight of the starry heavens upon his head, and his grey hair is frozen stiff with cruel cold. What need to tell of Tityus whose liver is ever renewed beneath the savage vulture's beak, to contend with his heavy punishment? Up, army of avengers, the hour is come at last, free the Titans from their chains; defend your mother. Here are seas and mountains, limbs of my body, but care not for that. Use them as weapons. Never would I hesitate to be a weapon for the destruction of Jove. Go forth and conquer; throw heaven into confusion, tear down the towers of the sky. Let Typhoeus seize the thunderbolt and the sceptre; Enceladus, rule the sea, and another in place of the sun guide the reins of dawn's coursers. Porphyrion, wreathe thou thy head with Delphi's laurel and take Cirrha for thy sanctuary."[75]

The destruction of the uprising of the Gigantes is understood to be a cataclysmic event, tearing islands asunder from the ocean floor, flinging mountains upon one another to be piled up to siege the heavens, radically altering the landscape of the inhabited Earth with the rage of Gaia and her newest children. While there would have been some understanding amongst Claudian and his audiences in late antiquity that earthquakes, volcanoes, and floods of bygone eras might be explained by the Gigantomachy, perhaps there is a subaltern reading of the text that can also be given. Perhaps it was one final paean of the polytheist past in light of the newly ascendant hegemony of Christianity: the children of Gaia, the Earth, who were in essence literally *pagani*, children of the rural soil against the citizen-soldiers of the Christian regime. They were called forth to defend their mother, and were in turn soundly defeated by the Olympians and their semi-divine offspring like Herakles. If Zeus can be likened to the Christian deity, then Herakles his semi-divine son can be likened to Jesus, and the whole of the Olympian generation can thus stand in for the new Christian dispensation, suppressing once and for all the children of the Earth in their last attempted uprising, in a time period late in the fourth century when the works of Julian the Philosopher to restore polytheism and the efforts of Flavius Eugenius and Arbogast in a similar direction were recent memories.

The twentieth and twenty-first centuries are very different than those earlier eras. From the late nineteenth century, Zeus' unquestionable supremacy has been undermined with the harnessing of electricity, and the Earth and our climate, as well as human societies, have suffered immeasurably due

> *the Earth Goddess in each generation of Greek Divine regimes is the source of the uprising which brings about the subsequent order and shapes the future era*

75   Maurice Platnauer (ed./trans.), *Claudian, Volume II* (Cambridge: Harvard University Press, 1922), pp. 280-283.

to all of the apparent "advances" achieved meanwhile, leaving stinking clouds in the air and cesspits of waste all across the earth, a new island of plastic in the Pacific that is no Atlantis resurfaced nor wandering Delos. Capitalism's excesses have collapsed "Works and Days" into a singular juggernaut that would make Hesiod—and I'd venture to say does make all of the Deities—groan with dismay and cry out with Their devotees for justice and peace. As in the Gigantomachy, the very surface of the earth and its geography is being altered daily from deglaciation, the melting of the polar icecaps, coastal flooding and unheard-of weather events, and the removal of mountaintops and clear-cutting of forests all in the name of the endless pursuits of Profit and Progress.

It is not that Zeus needs to be overthrown or destroyed on a Divine level; but that model of a perfect society over which He reigned is so far gone from our lived reality on Earth that it may as well never have existed. Perhaps it is the whispered words of Demeter in the ears of Demophoön that many of us hear at present, which causes us not only to rise up with Her as the unquiet voice of the raped Earth calling for justice in every area of human life, but also (and equally as important) to become those latter-day initiates into Her Mysteries—and those of many other Deities beyond number or reckoning from pantheons and cultures unknown to the Greeks and Romans, and perhaps even yet unknown to us at present—that will bring down the false Zeus imposed upon us by monotheistic hegemony and all of the destructive results it has wrought upon human societies, our individual minds and bodies, and the very substance which is the bodies of our Earth Goddesses Themselves.

P. Sufenas Virius Lupus

is the founder, Doctor, Magistratum, Sacerdos, and Mystagogos of the Ekklesía Antínoou—a queer, Graeco-Roman-Egyptian syncretist reconstructionist polytheist group dedicated to Antinous, the deified lover of the Roman Emperor Hadrian, and related divine figures. Lupus has been a practicing polytheist for 23+ years. Lupus is a metagender person, using Old Spivak pronouns (e, em, eir, eirs, emself), and has written seven books, plus many contributions to a variety of polytheist and pagan publications. E writes the Aedicula Antinoi blog and also contributes the "Speaking of Syncretism" column to Polytheist.com.

Nature's Rights
(Kadmus)

"...all, and only, humans have rights."[76]

"To give preference to the life of a being simply because that being is a member of our species would put us in the same position as racists who give preference to those who are members of their race."[77]

"Mother Earth and all its components, including human communities, are entitled to all the inherent rights recognized in this Law. The exercise of the rights of Mother Earth will take into account the specificities and particularities of its various components. The rights under this Act shall not limit the existence of other rights of Mother Earth."[78]

WHAT RIGHTS?

It may come as some surprise when I say this, but our understanding of what we mean by "rights" is a mess. There are few topics as important for political discourse and, I would claim, no topic as murky and confused in our thinking. In fact, I don't ultimately think that we have much grasp at all about what a right is or where it comes from. It is my suspicion, however, that a Pagan perspective brings surprising illumination to this problem. I hope, in this discussion, to offer some suggestions of how this might be the case.

---

76   Carl Cohen's view as presented by Tom Regan, *Animal Rights, Human Wrongs: An Introduction to Moral Philosophy* p. 112)

77   (Peter Singer *Practical Ethics*)

78   (*Law of Mother Nature* Article 5, Bolivian Law)

I think I can demonstrate to you the murky nature of rights talk fairly easily. Take a moment and attempt to explain to yourself directly what rights exist, where they come from, who has them, and why only those (neither more nor less) exist. Or, consider for a moment the interminable arguments that immediately occur whenever the question of a right's existence or non-existence comes up. Can you offer a clear and applicable principle that allows you to determine real from false rights?

Before I risk promoting too much confusion, allow me to limit the scope of our discussion. Rights can be divided into various categories, some easier to address than others. I will rely upon two fairly simple categories, though the seeming simplicity covers over some deep problems. Rights, for our purposes, can be **Natural** (or Universal, or Implicit, or Inalienable) or **Legal**. Natural rights are understood to exist in any context, free of any political framework or foundation, and are thus found everywhere despite temporal, cultural, or political differences. In turn, these natural rights are understood to legitimize political systems.

Legal rights, on the other hand, depend upon various political and legal structures for their existence. To offer a fairly simple example, life (or human life) is a fairly noncontroversial natural right, while the right to trial by jury is a legal right. Trial by jury cannot exist without a functioning political framework, and we could perhaps imagine other social forms to fulfill the legitimate demands of justice. However, trial by jury is a social and legal framework justified by its fulfillment of the demand offered by certain natural rights (i.e. life and liberty are supposedly insured by it, and so the natural rights provide the argument for the legal rights). So, legal rights are socially and historically contingent, but legitimated by natural rights that are not contingent.

You can see how this reliance of legal rights on natural rights functions by looking, for example, at key rulings by the Supreme Court of the United States of America. The ruling legalizing abortion (*Roe vs. Wade*) justifies the legal right to abortion by appeal to the "right to privacy" which, in turn, is understood as a subset of the natural right of liberty. The recent ruling legalizing marriage equality in all fifty states[79] bases a right to marriage on various rights such as

Take a moment and attempt to explain to yourself directly what rights exist, where they come from, who has them, and why only those (neither more nor less) exist.

self-expression—which again, ties back to the basic natural right of liberty.

Now, we can sometimes feel we have a pretty good grasp on what is and is not a right, because many of our legal rights are clearly delineated in political documents and processes. But this is hardly sufficient, especially since rights talk comes up most frequently when we are trying to address cases of systematic injustice in which the existing political framework, it is claimed, has failed in some way. The most powerful and important point, then, is where natural rights connect to and justify legal rights. This is also the ground most fought over. So, for example, people have argued for years following *Roe vs. Wade* that there is no right to privacy and so no right to abortion. Justice Scalia, in response to the recent marriage equality ruling, has argued that there is no right to self-expression and so no right to marriage.

Allow me to offer one further example of the contested connection between legal and natural rights. You can find arguments that there is a right to education and a right to healthcare. These rights are, in turn, vehemently rejected by others. The argument in favor of these rights relies often on natural rights. The rights to life and liberty are meaningless when one is dying of a curable disease or when one lacks the necessary education to make meaningful and effective choices in one's own life or in the political processes of one's community.

Of the flood of rights mentioned above (privacy, abortion, self-expression, marriage, healthcare, education), which do or do not exist, and why? This is a hard enough question for legal rights or those seemingly existing between nature and the law (privacy and self-expression for example), but things get worse when we go to the heart of the issue and ask which specific natural rights exist, why, and where they come from.

WHENCE RIGHTS?

In light of the standard practice of justifying legal rights by means of natural ones, our real topic here will be natural rights. My ultimate question is drawn from the quotation with which I opened this discussion. I wish to ask, "*Do only humans have rights?*" Or, as Ecuador and Bolivia have enshrined in their legal systems, does the earth itself have natu-

---

79 *Obergefell vs. Hodges*

ral inalienable rights? This would include the more narrow question of whether animals have rights, though I am just as interested in the question of the rights of plants, environments, mountains, seas and so on.

Considering my audience, I don't actually suspect I need to convince you that entities other than humans have rights (except, perhaps, for those of you who don't accept rights talk at all—a position for which there are some very strong justifications). However, I do suspect that we aren't nearly as clear about justifying our claims as we could be. So, I am not really preaching to the choir (or, better, coven). because I think the justification of our claims is what we need to focus on.

To figure out which natural rights exist and who or what can be a rights-bearer, it is necessary to come to some understanding of where these natural rights come from. The history of the concept of natural rights, at least in Western European thought, stretches from the Ancient Stoics, through medieval religious thought, to the modern social contract theorists such as John Locke, Jean Jacques Rousseau, Thomas Hutchinson, and Thomas Hobbes. Within this tradition we can find, roughly, four answers to the question of the origin of natural. I would like to briefly look at each of these in order to get a sense of their inadequacy.

REASON AS NATURAL LAW

The Stoics never actually argued for the existence of natural "rights" but they did argue for the **natural equality of all humans**. Their argument rested on several key elements. First, all nature was understood to be ordered according to an overarching order or law. Second, this law was divine and was identified as reason. Third, human reason was a privileged part of this divine natural order; in fact, reason made us partially divine.

This line of thought leads to two related conclusions. First, to the extent that we have reason, we are equal. This is the origin of the idea that natural rights are inalienable (in other words, we can never lose them). If you reflect on the idea of inalienability you can see it is a rather odd idea. Can't I be chained up? Or killed? Don't I lose my rights in these cases? The answer is "no". For the Stoics, and the "inalienable" tradition that follows from them, as long as we can reason we

are ultimately free. Even if my body is in chains, the most important part of me – my divine reason – is free. This, incidentally, provides the basis for some Stoics to actually support slavery and social inequalities of all sorts! Because what matters is reason, nothing social inequality does to us can touch our real freedom and equality. Many of the Stoics, as you might suspect, were surprisingly conservative in the outcome of their thought.

The second conclusion to be drawn from the Stoic view is that reason is the source of our knowledge of rights. This hooks up with inalienability to provide us with a test that can be applied to rights. If you think something is a natural right, ask whether it is inalienable. If it isn't, you have no right to it. In other words, nothing worth having can be lost and nothing we have a right to can be taken away. This view is also obviously anthropocentric and even falls short of providing rights to all humans since some lack reason. So, for the Stoics, **only, but not all, humans have rights** (with the addition of gods and any other entities with reason).

The development of these ideas leads to what we find in Locke and Thomas Jefferson. Natural rights are inalienable and uncovered by reason. Both reject the Stoic test as too limited, and instead rely upon the self-evidence of rights. We don't, in other words, need a test for what counts as a right because our natural rights are immediately apparent and obvious to the view of reason. Jefferson doesn't try to prove we have natural rights, he claims he doesn't need to. This has largely landed us in the mess we are today, with no system for determining what is or is not a right.

Jefferson and Locke also change the sense of inalienability used by the Stoics. For them, a natural right is inalienable because even if the practice of that right is taken away our claim to that right always remains. We always deserve and can demand life and liberty even when we are deprived of the use of them.

GOD

The Stoics, Locke, and Jefferson—as well as the long medieval tradition of natural law theory—all base the origin of rights on a certain conception of the divine. This conception is ultimately monotheistic (the Stoics believed in one ulti-

Jefferson doesn't try to prove we have natural rights, he claims he doesn't need to. This has largely landed us in the mess we are today, with no system for determining what is or is not a right.

mate divinity despite the existence of sub-deities) and anthropocentric (we occupy a special position at the head of most—or all—of nature due to our possession of reason and/or special selection by god).

It is important to stress that contemporary rights theory goes beyond the basis of God in very specific ways. First, natural rights do not rely upon a shared religious background for justification. Second, neither the Stoic nor Biblical god provides a basis for rejecting the social inequality of men and women or the practice of slavery. The Bible clearly supports slavery. In fact the New Testament, which was heavily influenced by Stoic thought, offers arguments in favor of slavery very similar to those found in Stoicism. Most go something like this: social distinctions are natural and divinely willed, so it is our duty to rationally fulfill the social roles and positions we find ourselves in, including the role of a slave. This allows both Stoics and the Biblical Paul to assert that a good slave must obey its master and so on. Locke followed the monotheistic reasoning underlying natural rights rather carefully and ended up arguing in favor of both American slavery and the wholesale theft of land from the Native Americans.

Finally, it should be noted that the longest use of divinely-ensured natural rights was to support the divine right of kings and firm social hierarchies. This shouldn't be surprising. I have often challenged my students to explain to me why a monarchical metaphysics with a divine all-powerful dictator should be compatible with anything other than a form of political tyranny. It's a difficult question and not one that all forms of Paganism can easily avoid.

NATURE

Interestingly, the history of natural rights theory hasn't been particularly focused on nature. Nature has seemed to require the underwriting of "nature's god" and/or reason. Despite that, we can detach something of an argument-from-nature from natural rights literature. We can derive from the thought of both Locke and Hobbes a sort of principle for deriving from nature a list of rights.

Rights would be, on this reading, those things which a living entity naturally feels are its own. So, in nature we fight for our life, our freedom of movement, our family, and things like food and shelter that we have gathered for ourselves.

The history of natural rights theory hasn't been particularly focused on nature. Nature has seemed to require the underwriting of "nature's god" and/or reason

Our instinctive defense of these things marks a natural knowledge of a right to them. From a traditional view, the failing of this thinking is obvious, since it doesn't set humans off from animals who also defend all these things, and for this reason it is more promising for us. Locke, deprived of his Biblical god and the superiority of reason, would be left with an argument like this alone. This can be expanded into a **capabilities view,** similar to that of Martha Nussbaum, that might assert that a natural entity has a right to develop its natural capabilities. Our sheer having-of-capabilities is a signal of a right to them and their expression/development.

PAIN AND PLEASURE – UTILITARIANISM

Strictly speaking, Utilitarians don't accept the existence of natural rights for various reasons, but we can talk of something very similar to a rights conception in Utilitarianism based on a limited type of capabilities view. For the utilitarian theorist only one thing is absolutely good, namely pleasure or happiness, and only one thing is absolutely bad, namely pain. This lays a universal obligation upon us to increase, as far as possible, the amount of pleasure or happiness in existence and to decrease the amount of pain. This is the basis of the argument by Peter Singer I quote from at the start of this discussion. Animals, as capable of pain and pleasure, are part of our obligation to lessen pain and increase pleasure, and might be said to have a right to this type of consideration. Animals have a right to have their suffering and happiness taken into account. Plants, mountains, seas, and so on are not obviously capable of pain or happiness and so do not enter into consideration beyond their instrumental relationship to animals and humanity.

NO NATURAL RIGHTS

I should add a consideration of the view that there are no natural rights. If we understand a right to mark a limit, a space or possession that cannot legitimately be invaded or taken away, then the following three views might be raised. Rousseau suggests that, since the state of nature is one of natural abundance and simplicity, no natural limits exist(or need exist) between people in nature. It is society that, giving rise to pride and greed, creates property, scarcity and domination and so necessitates rights. Hobbes argues something like the reverse: in the state of nature all entities have the power to do whatever they wish and so the right to do so. Because all action is a natural right for him, in this sense, then it makes no difference to say either that there are no natural rights or that everything is a natural right. Both lead to Hobbes' famous "war of all against all" in the state of nature. Finally, since the utilitarian thinks that we must balance the good of the greatest number of entities capable of happiness against any individual concerns, there are no predetermined limits protecting the life, liberty, capabilities or goods of any given individual. The majority, the famous "greatest number", might be said to have rights but no given individual does.

A PAGAN CONCEPTION OF RIGHTS

How can a Pagan perspective assist us in the challenge of making sense of the origin, nature and limits of rights? We don't have many historical precursors to work with. Much of Pagan history hasn't been particularly promising when it comes to individual freedoms or social equality—with rather important exceptions such as many Native American and traditional African cultures. Our strongest precursor might be taken to be the Stoics but, for many reasons, I do not take them to fit fully into a Pagan worldview. So, we can't really ask what Pagans have historically had to say about rights. Instead, we must take key elements of several forms of Paganism and attempt to work out their implications for natural rights theory.

The first thing we might note deals with the traditional derivation of natural rights from reason and god. The nature of the god in question leads almost inevitably to the focus on reason. For the Stoic, god and reason are all but indiscernible. In fact, the Stoics often called the universal divinity, universal law/reason, and human reason by the same Greek word – they called it the *Logos*. *Logos* is originally the Greek term for "word" but it came to mean reason amongst many other things. The Old Testament of the Bible reflects a similar view, whether through syncretism or chance, and the New Testament directly plagiarizes from the Stoic view.

Thus, in the Old Testament the god of the Bible **speaks** creation into existence and the Gospel of John starts with an almost entirely Stoic claim that "In the beginning was the *Logos*, and the *Logos* was with God, and the *Logos* was God." In this context the divine essence of reality will be located in the intellectual, rational, linguistic spheres of existence. This is also connected to the transcendent nature of a divinity external to creation, a transcendence that will frequently carry over into the rational part of humanity through a rejection of the body (and physical nature in general.)

The focus on reason and linguistic communities embodied in the natural rights tradition makes a very clear appearance in contemporary arguments about what can, and cannot, be a bearer of rights. Carl Cohen, a long-standing opponent of animal rights arguments, affirms that to have a right means to be able to assert a claim upon others while recognizing your own obligation to respond to their claims. In other words, only members of rational linguistic "moral communities" can be understood to have rights. It is clear to Cohen, though (not to many of his critics,) that only humans can make rational moral claims upon others and recognize those claims when they are made upon them. In other words, whether or not something has rights and what those rights are has everything to do with intellectual and linguistic capabilities.

In sharp contrast, consider the Pagan worldview of Hesiod's *Theogony*. In this origin story the cosmos arises out of the sexual and asexual bodily reproduction of families of gods. These gods, and the evolving universe they form through their reproduction, are largely inseparable from bodily nature. There is importantly a deep identity between much of nature and its divinities.

To cultures for which the divine is frequently also embodied and natural—rather than spiritually transcendent over nature—the world around us makes constant demands upon us in a manner very like the way traditional rights bearers do.

To appreciate the importance of this, ask yourself whether the Biblical god can be understood to have rights. It's an odd question because the answer is that the god of the Bible probably has all rights, or rather *absolute right*. What would this imply, then, for the rights of a natural world made up of gods in ever more various proportions and hierarchies? To cultures for which the divine is frequently also embodied and natural—rather than spiritually transcendent over nature—the world around us makes constant demands upon us in a manner very like the way traditional rights bearers do. Rivers and mountains, ancient trees and unplowed fields all make legitimate demands for various types of respect.

A Pagan theory of rights, then, will not be focused upon reason or a divine law-giver's plans and demands upon a tightly structured cosmic hierarchy. The hierarchy of divinities, cosmic forces, and realities within the Pagan worldview tend to be partly natural and partly political. Zeus, for example, plots and fights both to gain his position and to maintain it. Even his power, however, is tentative and maintained by the overall balance of politics amidst divinities and humans.

The overlap of nature and divinity in a Pagan view presents a unique opportunity—for once, we might fully turn to nature for guidance about the origin and extent of natural rights. What is more, it is clear that though our Pagan worldview might direct our attention to nature, we need not depend upon divine revelation or dictate for our understanding of rights. Paganism might teach us that nature is divine and lays demands upon us, but a Pagan faith is not necessary to accept the conclusions we can draw from this.

Let us conceive the cosmos, and all its subsystems from planets to seas to mountains and so on, to be living much as the Bolivian "Law of Mother Earth" does – in other words let us embrace Animism or pan-vitalism. We can begin to approach this by means of the capabilities view mentioned previously. We start with animals and plants, recognizing that each has a set of capabilities and impulses it seeks to express and fulfill. All things being equal (which, of course, they never are), each thing has an implicit right to pursue the path of its growth, life, and death. To put it as simply as possible, each thing has a right to exist.

But, despite the tendency towards what we might call biological chauvinism, not only organic entities express a nature and follow a path of development and change. All things individually express a type of nature and, collectively, take part in nestled interdependent systems. There is a Zen art dedicated to finding and appreciating examples of "perfect" stones, stones which best capture the nature of being a stone. These won't be polished gems or dramatic outcroppings, but rather simple stones that somehow express in an exemplary way the basic nature of being a stone. While any debate about what this nature is might be interminable, just like debates about the ultimate nature of humanity, it doesn't seem

While we often think about rights in terms of purely negative limits on the powers of others, rights go along with responsibilities and obligations.

absurd to attempt to better grasp what the nature expressed by stones (or any other natural entity) might be. It also doesn't seem absurd to suggest that when such a stone is ground into gravel or melted for industrial purposes, something has been lost and some wrong may have been done.

When I was a child my neighbors cut down an oak tree that had lived for several centuries. I cried inconsolably, filled with a sadness and anger that told me that something terrible had been done—an important obligation had been broken and an important good had been destroyed. Who were they to so casually dismiss an entity that was old before their ancestors had even come to this country? I recently went hiking in Prairie Creek Redwood State Park and there, amidst trees that were massive before the supposed birth of Christ, one can't help but feel an overpowering awe and need for respect and even worship. Not only do these entities have a right to exist, they have a dignity that goes along with an imperative that this be respected.

While we often think about rights in terms of purely negative limits on the powers of others, rights go along with responsibilities and obligations. A right to life or liberty demands that I respect these same rights in others. More than this, a right to life or liberty also lays an obligation on my shoulders to facilitate the living and freedom of others. It is not, as many libertarians might think, purely a right to be left alone and let everyone else alone in turn. Rights are expressions of communal membership, of being part of a dynamic system seeking to further its own development. Rights are the mark of our position in an environment, in nature. The sheer right that I have to my existence and self-development is mirrored in my obligation to protect and pursue the existence and self-development of the world of which I form a part.

Allow me to restate the previous points in a more schematic form for the sake of clarity. Informed by Paganism, but without need to rely upon it for justification, I argue that:

1. To the extent that animals fight for their lives and development they express a right to existence and self-expression.

2. Plants, similarly, strive to grow and survive, expressing the same right.

3. Even non-biological entities are self-sustaining systems that resist certain changes and, when they change, change in

a manner uniquely expressing their nature. So they, too, express a right to existence and self-expression.

4. Collectively, these elements form larger complex systems that, in turn, strive to change in various ways and resist other changes and so express the same natural claim to rights.

5. These rights are nestled, one within another, and interconnected such that no purely individual atomistic right to be left alone is feasible. Rather, rights imply collective responsibility and obligations one to another. Some entities fulfill or fail these obligations without rational thought or consciousness, others do not, but the distinction is not particularly important.

6. All existence is a drive to be, and to change, which assumes and must be granted a basic legitimacy.

Nature's Rights: The Model of Art

The philosopher Hans-Georg Gadamer argued that when a work of art is created, Being itself is increased. Similarly, sculptors frequently describe their work not as forcing material into some shape but rather as releasing and realizing the potential form that was already present in the material. The sculptor assists the object in its development and self-expression. Arguing for the rights of nature leads to some exceptionally difficult problems that the enriching nature of art might help us address.

If each thing (due to its sheer existence and path of development) has a right to exist, a libertarian understanding of rights might lead us into a rather striking form of nihilism. From this view, I can do nothing, can change nothing, without doing wrong. The ant I unknowingly tread upon today has been wronged.

There is something right, I would argue, about elements of this view. All existence comes at a price to those things existing around us and the ways most of us live today accentuate this price to unjust proportions. But, ultimately, the message of the rights of nature is not that all existence and action is wrong but rather that all existence and action comes with responsibility. As parts of an interwoven cosmos seeking to joyfully express its nature there is no exit from responsibility—we are, as Dostoyevsky puts it, "responsible for all to all". How can I eat and end the life of the entity devoured? Only with a firm acceptance of my obligation to express more fully in my life the potential of that entity and a respect for its sacrifice.

It may be that in some art the material is devoured, destroyed in the making, but in the best art – in the truest art – the material comes more fully to life and expression. Art is the act of freeing the potential of what is, of augmenting and nurturing the growth and expression of existence, and it is this that nature demands of us. Neither master and engineer nor illegitimate interloper, we are part of nature's living and called to take our part with loving devotion to the value of every other participant, be it tree, stone, bird or star.

This means, of course, an end to easy answers. If my interest is in having a nice clear list of forbidden actions and obligatory actions I am going to be much disappointed. We should not be surprised at this, as responsibility comes hand in hand with the obligation to think carefully and risk failure.

There is, at the most basic level, one natural right and it is shared by all things: the right to exist as a process of self-expression. It comes united with an obligation: the obligation to respect and assist the existence and self-expression of each thing around me. Sometimes this obligation will involve killing and destruction, but only in service to a greater expression of being. But most often it will involve nurturing and a loving service to the world and cosmos of which we are children.

> *There is, at the most basic level, one natural right and it is shared by all things: the right to exist as a process of self-expression. It comes united with an obligation: the obligation to respect and assist the existence and self-expression of each thing around me.*

An End to Easy Answers

We are concerned about rights because they represent, in our culture, an end to debate. They state "this far and no further," they draw an impassable line and are, in their, not up for vote or reform. Rights talk promises us clarity and simple easy answers. But, as my introduction to this essay should have suggested, when we need them most and are walking dangerous unclear ground our current theory of rights is obscure and ambiguous. Dream though we might of rights that end political debate, they have rather historically taken their source from political conflict and their recognition is the outcome, rather than the solution, of social conflict.

The view I have presented is complex, as it relies upon a universe of interrelated entities nestled one within another, each with a basic drive and right to fulfill that drive. The right to exist and to express one's existence through self-development is far from a bastion of easy direct answers. It motivates thought and responsibility and, more than ending debate, it *provokes* it. We can see this nowhere as clearly as on the topic of that most contentious of rights, the right to property. What does the right to existence and self-expression imply for the right to property? Most importantly, it implies that our concept of property and the right to it is deeply flawed.

Locke, and recent libertarian thinkers such as Robert Nozick, derive the right to property from the right to life (or existence, as I have been calling it). The idea is this: the right to life is a basic property right. I own my body and this body cannot be taken from me. This leads to the right to liberty, as my ownership over my body also means that my use of this body (with rather striking exceptions for Locke) cannot be limited. Now, when I work I use my body to transform something else. I invest some of my body—namely bodily energy and work—into the thing transformed. This makes the thing created part of my body in a limited sense. I have invested bodily life and so the thing becomes an extended part of my bodily life. When I work to grow apples my use of my body in the work makes the apples part of me in a very limited sense, so my basic right to ownership over my body extends to the thing produced. [80]

The view I have presented contains a different conception of both work and the natural world, largely because of the rejection of anthropocentrism. When I grow a tree it is as much the case that my body becomes part of the tree, part of its process of self-expression. The tree "owns" me just as much as I own it.

But, even the concept of ownership is off here. From a perspective that does not prioritize reason (and the mind-soul over the body and natural existence), I can't be said to own my body. I *am* my body, it is not property. Similarly, without anthropocentrism, we are not tempted to see the world as a collection of raw materials for use, such that I can imagine making the tree(or anything else) part of myself without any

thought to its own individual existence within an ever expanding complex of interconnected systems. The tree and I might be in partnership, but it does not become me and I do not become it. We are part of something larger, but neither dominates in the manner required for ownership. Furthermore, the tree is also in partnership with things other than myself that belies any claim to an exclusive relationship with it.

My right to self-expression includes my right not to have my partnerships unduly interfered with and broken. You can't come along and chop down the tree I have worked to grow without weighty reasons, but it is wrong to think that this entity with an existence and nature of its own is "mine" in any robust sense or that my relationship with it overpowers all other relationships it has. I have a right to have my relationships respected and protected, except when those relationships become unjustifiably abusive, dominating, or destructive. So, in an interconnected world viewed through the lens of the right to exist, the right to relationships replaces rights to property.

Kadmus

is a practicing ceremonial magician with a long standing relationship to the ancient Celtic deities. His interests and practice are highly eclectic but a deep commitment to paganism is the bedrock upon which they all rest. Kadmus is also a published academic with a Ph.D. in philosophy teaching at the college level.

---

80   Interestingly, this is also the basis of much Marxist thought mediated through Hegel's adoption of similar conceptions of work through which the world becomes an expression of the self and, as it were, a second body. It is also worth noting that this is the basis of Locke's argument in favor of taking land from the Native Americans. They didn't work the land, he claimed, and so didn't gain ownership through transformation of it.

Dirt Sorcery

Cropping/Gleaning

(Al Cummins)

'*Deserts, Woods, obscure Valleys, Caves, Dens, Holes, Mountains, or where men have been buried, Churchyards, &c. Ruined Buildings, Coal-mines, Sinks, Dirty or Stinking Muddy Places, Wells and Houses of Offices, &c.*'

Virtue

When the stars are distant, they glimmer; mirage-like, intangible, otherly. When the stars – in that sharp instant of meaning's bite – *matter* they may glitter. But what of the virtues of their starlight in the corners and detritus of the everyday and all-too-earthly? What of their *grit*?

In the words of dead men, Cornelius Agrippa explains that all actions and reactions upon the earth of the elemental world trace their origin to the Creator as mediated through the seven planets, which his teacher Trithemius was said to have referred to as 'the Secundarian Intelligencies'. This celestial reading of matter's inbuing of virtue speaks in a language of light, of suns, rays, and of that which Falls. To employ a more chthonic reading, to use planetary dirts is to employ the foot-tracks of the Wanderers. In the cropping there is doctoring, and in the milling of stony Saturn is the grist of the *ground*. Might we gather nourishment from the leftover harvest of the star's passing? How might we *glean*?

Just as we must reject divisive Cartesian dualism to situate our craft – our art and our medicine – in and from the body, so we might *nix* models of the isolated individual which deny the environmental engagements and inertias woven into selfhood. After all, such notions of self-made-manifest destiny allow the callous rugged individualism that carves the natural world into pieces for temporary profit, that hunts beauty from behind cross-hairs, and leave us only a glassy-eyed shell of a once-spirited world. Such mind-forged monocles perceive myopically and without depth, and allow powerful people to ignore those from whom their power derives, whose backs and bones are stolen and broken to build their pyramids.

To 'know thyself' in bespoke rings of orbiting engagements, *spinning* amidst a web of meanings, opportunities and interrelations, is to celebrate both roots and branches. This is a living understanding of how Alan Watts framed our origins: that we do not come into the world but emerge out of it. To *consider* environment and external factors upon the individual – metonymnically apprehended in the locative foci of place—is not to pigeonhole away our dove-winged agency. Rather than dumbly accept a layer of powerlessness, or settle for a set of excuses and chains, we might once more work the mirror both ways. Just as reflection allows the Above to narrate the Below in astrology, so can the Below be used to ground and quake different expressions in and of the Above in ritual magic. To work dirts for sorcery is to operationalise geographic astrological correspondences, to liberate them from fatalistic sociological prophecy or a hierarchy of cosmic obedience. As our surroundings influence us, so may we shape our destinies by stirring the envirtued earths harvested from sites of astral potency.

Here I echo the wisdom of Nicholaj De Mattos Frisvold and call sorcery the re-arranging of the *sortilege*, the manipulation of the parts of fate. In this sense, magicians – decent magicians, that is – not merely understand the world but change it.

Let us gather and consecrate our tools: by interment and exhumation, by the exchange of metals and the printed IOUs of absent gold. Burn the currency of hell. Clasp coins like plectrums to both dig and pluck at the grubby cracks and to leave respectfully. Pull brushes to gather fine powders into paper wraps, whose folds may be learned from the containment of seeds and less savoury but no less potent powders. Black ink, black clothes, black sky. All Saturn everything. For all earths are of Saturn: in the settling of ashes, in the turn of dust to dust, in every muddy stain, in the ooze and echoes down each *Cloaca Maxima*. A heavy, leaden, black Understanding of human life and death. A cradle of silence. To labour with Saturn's works is, in some sense, to live as a being not merely towards death, but within its very tide and time. While this certainly requires the operator to face hard dark truths, it need not only be considered morbid and malefic. Saturn is also the planet of mastery and *genius*, a star singing us our depth of thought and severity of action. It is the Wanderer furthest from the Sun, but thus nearest to the unknown; closest to the firmament and the body of the Queen of Heaven.

Thus the furthermost desolate old sites are a favourite of magical operators dealing with spirits of the wild, the untamed, the unclean. Blasted heaths that blur Elphame and Hades. Ancient monuments hacked and dragged from distant quarries by long-departed stone-cutters. Bronchiole boughs of skeletal trees breathing the winter's darkness. Susurrant forests whispering Mysteries of the Dead of the Night. Equally however, consider Satyrsdays: weekly Saturnalias of gallows humour and debauchery in the face of decay. To bury oneself alive and be uprooted screaming: whether in the *adust* burning manias that blacken our biles, the leaden foundations that pallor our complexions, or simply the heaviest of chemical beats and basement shadowslicks. To get primal. You might have dreamed about it.

SORROW

Let us engage in perhaps the most sanctioned form of gaining knowledge from the dead and conjure the shade of an historical example to visible appearance. We might consider the impact of the Thatcher government on British mining communities (often considered bastions of folk labour solidarity against Tory overrule, incidentally) at least rendered many sites in the UK doubly Saturnine; as they are mostly now both mines *and* ruins. Emptied village pubs became headstones to workless people buried under sell-offs, privatisations, redundancy, alcoholism, depression, and the night-sticks of bussed-in police strikebreakers. The graves of the pits unmarking generations of earth-workers betrayed. Ancestral shades wiped away as grubby coal-dust smudges. Roots salted.

ruins are by no means the preserve of the industrial, or indeed the old rural. If wilderness is wherever you can get lost, wherever there is danger, wherever is allowed to sink from memory; certainly they can be found in cities.

But ruins are by no means the preserve of the industrial, or indeed the old rural. If wilderness is wherever you can get lost, wherever there is allowed to sink from memory; certainly they can be found in cities. Sites of urban poverty and deprivation are places of Saturn. The crossroads that go nowhere, boarded-up residences, road blocks, burned-out bus-stops, the demarcations of red-lining, the echoing vaults of food banks, the broken windows of blinded buildings; the sites that wordlessly en-grave the visible lacks of opportunity and the oppressive absence of what was supposed to trickle down. The moss grown upon the temples of the skull of Jane Jacobs.

Indeed, it seems the gnawing hungers of poverty cannot be approached without an explicit commitment to understanding the shadows of the polis. Recalling the Hebrew origins of the word *ghetto* might remind us of the *Picatrix*'s attribution of Judaism as the religion of Saturn: which is also, of course, the Black planet. The bloody libels that historically elided Sabbath and Sabbat – and certainly the comparison of old Kronos' defeat by noble Zeus in Christian supercessionism – were powerful weapons of anti-Semitism. Similarly, the humoural theories that sought to apprehend and treat melancholy were roped in to argue African complexions were a punishment for the shameful lasciviousness of sons of Noah, enshrining pale European skin as the original zenith of humanity – closer to the image of a luminous Bright White Creator – and expressly theologising colourism. Saturn sings scapegoat songs of the accused and the oppressed: the *denigrated*. And Saturn's potent virtue can be harnessed by those suffering under its conditions for protection and defence. To apprehend and obliterate the darkness of hatred and oppression is its own deep Saturnine mystery. Moreover, I believe those wan who stand with our Black siblings should hear in Saturn's silence an entreaty to speak less and listen more.

To apprehend and obliterate the darkness of hatred and oppression is its own deep Saturnine mystery.

The people of Saturn are graveyard-shift labourers, toilers in the dark, sweepers of soiled passages, office workers exchanging time for coin in minimums, bearers of palls, dusting broom-men, hollowers and the hollowed-out, delvers, those with dirt under their nails. We might also recall one of the many radical sects to emerge from the world turned upside down of the English Revolution, who sought to make the wastelands grow as a treasured and universally-shared commonwealth, and who called themselves Diggers. The foot-tracks of such Saturnsfolk across time and space plant the planet's seeds of action.

To our Saturnine litany of subterranean locales one might add the chthonic aspects of the underground transit, and perhaps particularly the abandoned underhalls of closed 'ghost stations'. One might leave prayers and offerings: the roots of plants, old coins, stones, the heraldry of the dead and the gnomes. It is worth pointing out that the Underground of London Below, with its historied layers of habitation, feels very different from the underworld of the NYC subway. The former is a labyrinth of carriages rattling past Roman soldiers nestling against the poor nameless of early modern plague pits and Victorian sex workers, as new line construction labourers unearth the skulls of Bedlamites. The latter is cars brushing past a thin patina of concentrated set-

tlement to the bones of the Earth itself, at once simultaneously more modern and ancient.

With apt finality, however, the main Saturnine sites are the haunts of the dead: graveyards, funeral homes and crematoria as well as churchyards. Consider not merely the earths of graves themselves, but the dirts of boneyard gates, memorial statues, high crosses, and solitary paths and junctions. The yews lining the way, the barrow, the mausoleum, the fence, the hill; each has their own paths and potentials. Dirts encasing desiccated dead flora and fauna can assist in an underworld tour, and themselves *mori* a *memento* of mortality.

Furthermore the dirts gathered from economic ghost-towns, fragments of pavements from sides no longer walked, rust from forgotten street-names and signposts mouthing bitter everythings to the stopped pulses of traffic, have another order of necromantic applications. They offer crossroads for meeting unliving *genius loci*. There is a weight of death in the sites of private, and especially privatised, privation that cities keep like secrets.

WORKS

It is entirely soberingly reasonable to be overwhelmed by the particular ecological, economic and political sorrows of our present modern World: our skies, earths and seas are poisoned; extinctions are common enough to need rates; capitalism's wealthy exacerbate new extremes of poverty, banishing blackened masses to an incarceration of hunger, disease, and death. But if our dirt sorceries can perform any effective work, it may be at least to transmute our sorrows into earth-shattering Works. Perhaps no sickle can cut a path through the cashcropped rapeseed monoculture back to the Garden, but *ultimately* we must still work with and in the dark Earth.

By the understanding of geomancy, we can conceive of works of Saturn as radically rooted in binding and sorrow. The figures of *Carcer* and *Tristitia* meet at a point of fortification, where deathly Saturn is found in the hush of heavy foundational matters: prevention, barricades and the heavy presence of absence. Both *Weltschmerz* and the stasis of depression. The limitations and threnodies of mortality.

Carcer *defines* acts of separation and imprisonment. Ideographically, these are workings of the cell that encircles; that which contains and constrains, encloses and enslaves, preserves and protects. An eternal circle. Container spells – from witch bottles to charm bags – all operate at least partially on such Saturnine mechanics. Such container spells are also often buried, walled off, or otherwise hidden. Saturn is discrete and discreet.

By separation, there is nullification, a removal from the world – whether physical, mental, social or emotional. Furthermore, there is a *decline*: a refusal and a descent, even a katabasis. Isolation may remove distractions and can focus and concentrate. By the silence and silencing of this planet there are works of stillness, the softness of dust and the encumbrance of deep time. The writer's desk and the jail-cell. The blackest eclipsing ink from which light cannot escape.

Tristitia wails of melancholy and grieving, of lamentation, of *howling*. In its glyph of a depression, we may see a pit or a stake driven into the ground, which was the manner in which premodern suicide victims were tragically disposed of at crossroads. It gravely marks both a mournful remembrance of the past and a bleak anguish in facing the future.

> *Isolation may remove distractions and can focus and concentrate. By the silence and silencing of this planet there are works of stillness, the softness of dust and the encumbrance of deep time. The writer's desk and the jail-cell. The blackest eclipsing ink from which light cannot escape.*

We might read it as both the veil of tears and the Buddha's bodhi tree, each shading a meditation upon the nature of suffering. It is the tragedy that inspires compassion, as well as the overwhelming despair that might carry us away from the world. Navigating the necessary funeral rites of grief and remembrance for the bereaved – not to mention preparation of the deceased for their further journeys – upon and under the waves of sorrow, with its thanatos-tides pulling toward oblivion, is an unliving lesson. Saturn's dark sea swells from bitter tears.

Earth wetted with such tears may nurture spectral trees, however. Some greencrafts teach dried herbs are themselves dead, and thus prefer working the fresh living plants for their vivifying and potent sap-blood. Yet Saturn's shadow flies on raven wings through the realms of Death, Time, Remembrance and Agriculture, to *lead* us – as the corvid flies – to potent techniques from precisely this perspective. Between the *solve* of the crop and the *coagula* of the glean, there is indeed doctoring.

The Sea-goat and Water-bearer both have powerful relation to Binah's amniotic and funerary Sea, the Single Sea of the Mourning Woman, the Sorrowful Mother, who brings forth death and life. Their natures of Earth and Air vocalise a return to the dirt, black magic in the soil and the sigh, breath and bone.

ABUNDANCE

One of the oft-overlooked features of early modern European astrological sorcery is the combination of two planetary forces. We also see this in the utilities of the entire spectrum of planetary hours of Saturnsday, offered in grimoires such as the *Hygromanteia* and other tomes of occult philosophy. These bi-planetary preparations and workings can take the form of gathering Saturnine dirts at other planetary hours, or even in combining dirts from each planet. Dust, a precipitate of time, gathered from other planetary locations offers a readily available crux of Saturnine materia and other astral virtues.

Consider the virtues of Saturn and Jupiter when combined, rather than embattled as in titanic struggles with powers of the past. Their most obvious application might well be in magically affecting court case works of incarceration, but they might also be utilised in a working to shroud or bind the law. The *Hygromanteia* lists a Jupiterian hour of Saturnsday as good for 'performing necromancy'; drawing to mind the honoured and honourable ancestors, Hades' title as 'Terrestrial Jove', and even perhaps (given Jupiter's older associations with medicine) an ennobling ancestral healing. Similarly, the twin qualities of study and elevation speak of works of education, and wisdom as right action in the world.

Conjoined with Mars, the Greater and Lesser Malefics together wreak harm and misfortune. Make no mistake, there are deep poisoned wells to draw from in Saturnine workings. Mars' hot-blooded explosively wrathful ire combined with Saturn's cold calculating bitter and begrudged revenge is a potent, violent, deathly alloy. At the crux of the red and black meet Four Horsemen of Death, War, Famine and Pestilence who might each or all be loosed upon enemies along these paths.

Likewise combinatory workings with the Sun might be used 'to attack those in power'. Magical use of Saturnine dirts can confront elites with the results of their actions, inactions and ignorances. Trails may be laid to encourage attention and resources to forgotten ruins of industry and residence, or fortify against foreclosures and eviction notices. The conjunction of Saturn and Sol also conjures works vacillating between light and dark, hidden and revealed; the hit-and-run of the guerrilla tactics, as activists melting from the shadows to throw flaming torches, scrawl quotes from Robert Taber's *War of the Flea* on the enclosure walls, and melt back into the night. The open letters of Subcommandante Marcos of the Zapatistas speak of many uses of masks and mirrors to speak truth to power in the silence of the dead.

Saturnine-Venusian workings beget fear and hatred through agents of disgust, debauch and despair. Once initiated in the *nigredo* depths, however, putrefaction – life crawling from fertile death – might be harnessed in the birthing of monsters, the distillation of poisons, Elusinian separations and reunions. In these separations, we might also find the frenzies of dismembering maenads or the seven swords that pierce the heart of Our Lady of Sorrow, our one polymorphously perverse womb and tomb, our bittersweet oceanic Graal.

Psychopompous Mercury finds strong forms of work through underworldly Saturn, in cursing and fortifying infrastructures, in impeding and releasing impediments on travel over, across and under the earth. This union of chthonic currency has also been considered 'for finding a useful treasure'. Likewise, secrets and their discovery, even their flight upon parrot-wings of bad news and slander, are a further form of working involving the buried and unearthed. Such operations might be further employed for keeping others in the dark, grounding lines of communication, blacking out passages, and otherwise clotting the blood of circulation.

Just as with the other Luminary, Saturn and the Moon regard each other across a polarity. Rather than vacillating however, they are enthroned as the most ponderous and alacritous Wanderers respectively, holding sway over all things between them. Together they might hold clock-hands in workings concerning Time and the slipping *grains* of the hourglass. They might also move as distinguishing the brief lives and lingering shades left by mortality, the Moon

alighting sciomantic mysteries and works of waning. For the Moon is the portal through which far-darting three-formed Soteria, mistress of *daimones* and restless dead, ensouls the world. It is gravely apt that these two stars, these two torches of the Night, are scheduled 'for speaking with demons' and learning the language of skeletons. It goes without saying – tonguelessly one might (not) say – that there is a lunacy in discovering what skulls grin about.

With sombre finality, we should consider the very haunting of planetary locations by the sorcerer is one manner in which one becomes more like the planet, how one attuned and refines oneself toward those planetary mysteries. The magic is in the process of journeying to these sites, performing our gathering rituals of collection and consecration, not to mention those of recompense and gratitude. The sorcery is in part in the enchantment of presence and involvement in and around the location. It is not simply the *materia* itself, but learning something of its source, and exposing oneself to those places of power. The operator is empowered through a *terroir* of ritual itself, which renders sorcery always a site-specific Art.

The attitudes for gathering the dirts of Saturn are hungry, tearful, humble before death, poor before power, rude, base and profane, *crowing*. Upright as a tombstone. Quiet as the grave.

Al Cummins

is an Anglo-Irish Midlander, necromancer, and occasional supply teacher. He's just finished a PhD on early modern magic and the passions and moved to New York, and did both because Love. He mainly works goetia, grimoires, seventeenth-century England, hoodoo, and a pretty damn fine chana paneer jalfrezi

Joy Against the Machine

Ned Ludd

(Yvonne Aburrow)

The machines must be fed constantly
not just with oil – they take the arms and fingers
of those who tend them. They invade the dreams
of the workers, who hear their clattering
even in the furthest reaches of sleep.
So we creep by night into factories.
Ned Ludd – general of the armies of night –
is with us. His strength was in my arm
when I smashed the machine loom, smashed and smashed.
Strength like the grip of ivy, crushing
stone and metal. The power of roots is in him,
relentlessly pushing up from the earth.
He is the land fighting back, rising up.
against the encroaching iron and steel.

Yvonne Aburrow

Yvonne Aburrow has been a Pagan since 1985 and a Wiccan since 1991. She has an MA in Contemporary Religions and Spiritualities from Bath Spa University, and lives and works in Oxford, UK. Her most recent book is All Acts of Love and Pleasure: inclusive Wicca. She has also written four books on the mythology and folklore of trees, birds, and animals, and two anthologies of poetry. She is genderqueer, bisexual, and has been an anarchist socialist green leftie feminist for the last thirty years.

The Soul is a Site of Liberation (Anthony Rella)

PROTRACTED PERILS

At my first post-graduate mental health job, my program sponsored a clinical training in a therapeutic modality called Prolonged Exposure Therapy (PE). The trainers, coming from a military background, presented this modality as one used with active duty soldiers and veterans who are suffering from post-traumatic stress disorder (PTSD). The thrust of PE is to directly confront the stresses of having one's trauma response triggered until the traumatic memories are integrated and the triggers decrease in intensity. There are a few pieces to this work, but the primary modality is identifying the client's most traumatic or distressing memory and telling the story to the therapist, over and over and over again.

This may sound horrifying. Nearly every successful treatment of PTSD at some point includes confronting triggers and retelling trauma stories. The theory is that re-experiencing trauma memories and arousal is the brain's natural method of integrating and overcoming it; while in PTSD, the pathology is that the sufferer gets caught in a cycle of avoidance and re-experiencing, neither able to integrate or deny the trauma. PE strips down the therapy to psycho-education and exposure. Sessions one and two are about explaining trauma and the reasons for PE, and from the third session onward it is primarily exposure. PE is an economical treatment, promising significant relief from PTSD in 8-12 sessions, which might be less than two months if multiple sessions happen per week. Our trainers explained that PE has been used successfully to heal active duty soldiers so that they can go back out on the front lines in a short span of time.

How wonderful! Now we can quickly dispense with the inconvenient psychic costs of battle so we can plug our soldiers back into the machine of endless war.

According to the therapist guide for PE by Foa, Hembree, and Rothbaum, PE reduced symptoms for a group of ten veterans by 58% on the mean. David J. Morris, a veteran writing for Slate.com, reports that these and other statistics of success obscure some of the less desirable possible outcomes of PE in his July 21, 2015 article "Trauma Post Trauma":

> "The problem with prolonged exposure is that it also has made a number of veterans violent, suicidal, and depressed, and it has a dropout rate that some researchers put at more than 50 percent, the highest dropout rate of any PTSD therapy that has been widely studied so far."[81]

As it is designed, PE launches the client into exposure so quickly that many clients are unlikely to feel they have a safe and trusting relationship with their therapist. Even my PE trainers admitted that it was common for clients to no-show session three because they knew they would begin exposure.

ESTABLISHMENT ATTESTATIONS

PE is one of many psychotherapy models promoted by the economic and cultural push for efficient, low-cost, and "evidence-based" treatments. "Evidence-based" care is one of the more recent trends in mental healthcare, driven by the marriage of scientific inquiry and market forces marshaled by insurance agencies. Contextualized within the scientific-medical model, the vision is to develop therapies that accurately identify symptoms and reduce or eliminate them with targeted, precise, economical interventions. This is far afield of the older model of two to three sessions of psychoanalysis weekly for years with the goal of personality reconstruction. In principle, the evidence-based drive seems ethical. It allows providers to be held accountable for providing treatment that has demonstrated effectiveness.

Psychology, being a soft science, has a strange relationship with research. Few studies on counseling strategies employ a strict application of scientific research models because many variables cannot be controlled without ethical violations. First of all, you need to find a large sample size of people who are not receiving any psychological support and whose primary problem is the illness being studied. This is a difficult task in itself, especially for problems like trauma that are frequently complicated by substance abuse and other environmental or interpersonal problems. Secondly, one cannot ethically take a group of that sample and keep them as a control, receiving no treatment. Researchers often solve this problem by giving the control group a pseudo-treatment like "supportive listening." Morris cites Bruce Wampold describing how PE's use of supportive listening for research was problematic:

> "The 'supportive' therapists could only respond warmly; the patients were not allowed to talk about their trauma, were directed to talk about other current problems, and were given no therapeutic actions intended to help them. No decent therapist would ever treat a victim of rape in that way."

This particular research would not demonstrate PE's effectiveness over other kinds of competently executed therapy. We mostly see that PE is superior to shitty therapy.

An article published on the Substance Abuse and Mental Health Services Administration (SAMHSA) by Norcross and Lambert states that the strength of the therapeutic relationship is a factor equal to the treatment modality in contributing to the best outcome for clients[82]. That is, treatment is likely to fail if the therapist cannot develop a strong working relationship with the client, no matter how effectively and precisely they apply their evidence-based practice. A strong alliance includes the therapist's ability to collaborate with the client rather than force an agenda; their ability to respond to the client with warmth and equanimity even when the client is ambivalent or hostile; their genuineness in the relationship; and their ability to accurately empathize with the client's experience. When working with a client who has been failed, neglected, abused, or exploited by their caregivers and systems at large, building a strong relationship can take years.

From a Jungian psychoanalytic perspective, what is called mental illness is the psyche's attempt to compensate, cure, or

From a Jungian psychoanalytic perspective, what is called mental illness is the psyche's attempt to compensate, cure, or transform a problem that the ego cannot solve.

---

81   Norcross, J. & Lambert, M. (2010). Evidence-based therapy relationships. Substance Abuse and Mental Health Service Administration.
http://www.nrepp.samhsa.gov/pdfs/Norcross_evidence-based_therapy_relationships.pdf

82   Morris, D. (2015). Trauma post trauma. Slate.com

transform a problem that the ego cannot solve. "Symptoms" in this context are productive, creative responses to a different problem. Treatment focused primarily on making the symptoms go away would thus be ineffective in the long-term, as the problem to which the symptoms are responding would continue to exist. We might theorize on this in the case of a person who is suffering from substance abuse and PTSD. The substance abuse might be their attempt to "solve" the problem of distress from their constantly being triggered, which is itself the psyche's attempt to "solve" the problem of integrating and healing from their trauma.

Jungian therapy, incidentally, is a kind of therapy for which it is difficult to make evidence-based research, because it is not easily operationalized like PE or Cognitive-Behavioral Therapy is. "Operationalized" essentially means broken down into a recipe, or a mechanistic series of behaviors that one can observe and replicate. Therapies that are more humanistic, improvisational, intuitive, and responsive to the human beings in the room do not easily become reduced to flat models that one can replicate over and over again, and truly few therapists I know who work with evidence-based therapies actually apply the model rigidly. People generally do not go along with those kinds of agendas; either they unconsciously rebel against them, or they encounter bumps in life that need more attention than following the prescribed path.

The therapist's theoretical orientation or choice of treatment modality is in some ways more important for the therapist than it is for the client. A firm orientation keeps the therapist grounded in their role, able to filter out what personal thoughts or feelings are not useful to share with the client; and focuses how the therapist attends to and intervenes with the client. Therapeutic modality and orientation is what makes the relationship a therapeutic one, rather than just another messy interpersonal affair. What heals is the deep human connection that therapy allows, with all of its potency focused on helping the client to be with their own experience, know themselves, and heal. What therapy needs is a relationship with the soul, and the soul is cast out when we try to make therapy operationalized, efficient, and economical.

Depression may not be merely an obstacle to being the best middle manager you can be; depression may well be trying to get you to see how much you fucking hate being a middle manager

THE EGO AND THE SOUL

We need a strong ego to manage our lives effectively, and some forms of mental illness make the waters of the soul too stormy for an ego to find the stability it needs. This is one of the benefits of psychotropic medications that afford some people needed perspective to live. Western cultures, however, have valorized heroic egoism and disconnected from our roots in the soul. The myths of "pulling one's self up by one's bootstraps," overcoming adversity without help from anyone, a human's value only being what they are capable of producing or consuming—all reinforce the position of Ego as Gnostic Demiurge, floating in the darkness and looking at the worlds both intoxicated by its belief in its endless power, overwhelmed with loneliness and insecurity, and unable or unwilling to hear the voice of Wisdom behind crying out, "You are not alone! Turn around!"

Disconnected from its roots in the non-rational domains of the psyche, ego looks at life as a series of problems to overcome or challenges to beat down. Ego centralizes its plans, goals, and desires and wants to drive forward at all costs. Feeling too tired to finish that report? Don't take a nap, chug a Monster energy drink. Feeling sad and lonely? Don't mess around with that shit—drink some booze, go find someone to fuck. Feeling sort of empty and dissatisfied with life and somewhat guilty that others around you suffer while you strive to be the 1%? Well, fuck those suffering people, they probably deserve it.

All of these "solutions" keep the ego centralized, but the "problems" are arguably coming from the larger, deeper Self. Sadness, loneliness, and emptiness are emotional information that tell us something about our deep wants and needs. Emotions do not speak the language of reason, they need the rational mind to humble itself enough to strive to learn their language. Emotions are wedded closely to the needs and desires of body and soul, the animal and divine parts of ourselves that in many ways are always free. As much as we try to regulate and control them with substances, those parts of us will only become louder and more insistent until either they kill us or we listen to them.

In some ways the process is like what happens on a grander scale in our relationship with the environment. If we had listened to the warnings of climate change experts thirty years ago we might have spared ourselves a hard road ahead; instead, we avoided the hard lessons and corrections that will be necessary and now climate change is accelerating, eventually to force us to make the changes we could have made voluntarily.

The soul is autonomous and integral to who we are. Psychotherapy is a practice of recovering from distressing experiences, and it has a heritage and potential to be a practice of liberation. Therapists and clients work together to bridge the ego and the soul, to discover the value in every facet of the Self and bring those into better working relationships. Depression may not be merely an obstacle to being the best middle manager you can be; depression may well be trying to get you to see how much you fucking hate being a middle manager and how much you compromise yourself and your values every day to play nice, appease others, and strive for that elusive feeling of security and stability that is guaranteed to no one. PTSD in a veteran may in part be their psyche's revolt against the tasks assigned to them by their service to government and unjust wars of empire.

I become increasingly suspicious of the kind of inner dialogue that begins with, "I guess I need to just..." When we rehearse that speech to ourselves over and over, we are not really listening to what the body and soul need. We have come up with an intellectual explanation of what is happening with a similarly intellectual action plan for what needs to happen, but that does not engage the wants and needs of the body and heart, and thus those plans often fail.

The soul does not care for our external accomplishments, a forty-hour work week, a Ferrari, or a trophy spouse. The soul invites us to deepen into the soul of the world, with all of its suffering and unfolding evolution. The soul invites us to slow down, to listen to the heart and body, to feel with one's animal self what is missing or what action is needed. The soul does not want us to turn away from outrage or injustice but to look at the pleasures and pains of the world together. The soul is a dangerous thing to take seriously. It is the space wherein Gods dwell, the container for Spirit, ever transforming and never resting. The soul is a site of liberation.

Anthony Rella

is a witch, writer, and therapist living in Seattle, Washington. Anthony is a student and mentor of Morningstar Mystery School, and has studied and practiced witchcraft since starting in the Reclaiming tradition in 2005. Professionally, he is a psychotherapist working full-time for a community health agency and part-time in private practice.

In Praise of the Dancing Body

(Silvia Federici)

The history of the body is the history of human beings, for there is no cultural practice that is not first applied to the body. Even if we limit ourselves to speak of the history of the body in capitalism we face an overwhelming task, so extensive have been the techniques used to discipline the body, constantly changing, depending on the shifts in labor regimes to which our body was subjected to. Moreover, we do not have one history but different histories of the body: the body of men, of women, of the waged worker, of the enslaved, of the colonized.

A history of the body then can be reconstructed by describing the different forms of repression that capitalism has activated against it. But I have decided to write instead of the body as a ground of resistance, that is the body and its powers - the power to act, to transform itself and the world and the body as a natural limit to exploitation.

There is something we have lost in our insistence on the body as something socially constructed and performative. The view of the body as a social [discursive] production has hidden the fact our body is a receptacle of powers, capacities and resistances, that have been developed in a long process of co-evolution with our natural environment, as well as inter-generational practices that have made it a natural limit to exploitation.

By the body as a 'natural limit' I refer to the structure of needs and desires created in us not only by our conscious decisions or collective practices, but by millions of years of material evolution: the need for the sun, for the blue sky and the green of trees, for the smell of the woods and the oceans, the need for touching, smelling, sleeping, making love.

This accumulated structure of needs and desires, that for thousands of years have been the condition of our social reproduction, has put limits to our exploitation and is something that capitalism has incessantly struggled to overcome.

Capitalism was not the first system based on the exploitation of human labor. But more than any other system in history, it has tried to create an economic world where labor is the most essential principle of accumulation. As such it was the first to make the regimentation and mechanization of the body a key premise of the accumulation of wealth. Indeed, one of capitalism's main social tasks from its beginning to the present has been the transformation of our energies and corporeal powers into labor-powers.

In Caliban and the Witch (2004) I have looked at the strategies that capitalism has employed to accomplish this task and remold human nature, in the same way as it has tried to remold the earth in order to make the land more productive and to turn animals into living factories. I have spoken of the historic battle it has waged against the body, against our materiality, and the many institutions it has created for this purpose: the law, the whip, the regulation of sexuality, as well as myriad social practices that have redefined our relation to space, to nature, and to each other.

Capitalism was born from the separation of people from the land and its first task was to make work independent of the seasons and to lengthen the workday beyond the limits of our endurance. Generally, we stress the economic aspect of this process, the economic dependence capitalism has created on monetary relations, and its role in the formation of a wage proletariat. What we have not always seen is what the separation from the land and nature has meant for our body, which has been pauperized and stripped of the powers that pre-capitalist populations attributed to it.

Nature has been inorganic body and there was a time when we could read the winds, the clouds, and the changes in the currents of rivers and seas. In pre-capitalist societies people thought they had the power to fly, to have out-of-body experiences, to communicate, to speak with animals and take on their powers and even shape-shift. They also thought that they could be in more places than one and, for example, they could come back from the grave to take revenge of their enemies.

Not all these powers were imaginary. Daily contact with nature was the source of a great amount of knowledge reflected in the food revolution that took place especially in the Americas prior to colonization or in the revolution in sailing techniques. We know now, for instance, that the Polynesian populations used to travel the high seas at night with only their body as their compass, as they could tell from the vibrations of the waves the different ways to direct their boats to the shore.

Fixation in space and time has been one of the most elementary and persistent techniques capitalism has used to take hold of the body. See the attacks throughout history on vagabonds, migrants, hobo-men. Mobility is a threat when not pursued for work-sake as it circulates knowledges, experiences, struggles. In the past the instruments of restraint were whips, chains, the stocks, mutilation, enslavement. Today, in addition to the whip and the detention centers, we have computer surveillance and the periodic threat of epidemics as a means to control nomadism.

Mechanization—the turning of the body, male and female, into a machine—has been one of capitalism's most relentless pursuits. Animals too are turned into machines, so that sows can double their littler, chicken can produce uninterrupted flows of eggs, while unproductive ones are grounded like stones, and calves can never stand on their feet before being brought to the slaughter house.

I cannot here evoke all the ways in which the mechanization of body has occurred. Enough to say that the techniques of capture and domination have changed depending on the dominant labor regime and the machines that have been the model for the body.

Thus we find that in the 16 and 17th centuries (the time of manufacture) the body was imagined and disciplined according to the model of simple machines, like the pump and the lever. This was the regime that culminated in Taylorism, time-motion study, where every motion was calculated and all our energies were channeled to the task. Resistance here was imagined in the form of inertia, with the body pictured as a dumb animal, a monster resistant to command.

With the 19th century we have, instead, a conception of the body and disciplinary techniques modeled on the steam engine, its productivity calculated in terms of input and output, and efficiency becoming the key word. Under this regime, the disciplining of the body was accomplished through dietary restrictions and the calculation of the calories that a working body would need. The climax, in this context, was

> Mechanization -- the turning of the body, male and female, into a machine -- has been one of capitalism's most relentless pursuits.

the Nazi table, that specified what calories each type of worker needed. The enemy here was the dispersion of energy, entropy, waste, disorder. In the US, the history of this new political economy began in the 1880s, with the attack on the saloon and the remolding of the family-life with at its center the full-time housewife, conceived as an anti-entropic devise, always on call, ready to restore the meal consumed, the body sullied after the bath, the dress repaired and torn again.

In our time, models for the body are the computer and the genetic code, crafting a dematerialized, dis-aggregated body, imagined as a conglomerate of cells and genes each with her own program, indifferent to the rest and to the good of the body as a whole. Such is the theory of the 'selfish gene,' the idea, that is, that the body is made of individualistic cells and genes all pursuing their program a perfect metaphor of the neo-liberal conception of life, where market dominance turns against not only group solidarity but solidarity with own ourselves. Consistently, the body disintegrates into an assemblage of selfish genes, each striving to achieve its selfish goals, indifferent to the interest of the rest.

To the extent that we internalize this view, we internalize the most profound experience of self-alienation, as we confront not only a great beast that does not obey our orders, but a host of micro-enemies that are planted right into our own body, ready to attack us at any moment. Industries have been built on the fears that this conception of the body generates, putting us at the mercy of forces that we do not control. Inevitably, if we internalize this view, we do not taste good to ourselves. In fact, our body scares us, and we do not listen to it. We do not hear what it wants, but join the assault on it with all the weapons that medicine can offer: radiation, colonoscopy, mammography, all arms in a long battle against the body, with us joining in the assault rather than taking our body out of the line of fire. In this way we are prepared to accept a world that transforms body-parts into commodities for a market and view our body as a repository of diseases: the body as plague, the body as source of epidemics, the body without reason.

Our struggle then must begin with the re-appropriation of our body, the revaluation and rediscovery of its capacity for resistance, and expansion and celebration of its powers, individual and collective.

Dance is central to this re-appropriation. In essence, the act of dancing is an exploration and invention of what a body can do: of its capacities, its languages, its articulations of the strivings of our being. I have come to believe that there is a philosophy in dancing, for dance mimics the processes by which we relate to the world, connect with other bodies, transform ourselves and the space around us.

From dance we learn that matter is not stupid, it is not blind, it is not mechanical, but has its rhythms, has its language, and it is self-activated and self-organizing, Our bodies have reasons that we need to learn, rediscover, reinvent. We need to listen to their language as the path to our health and healing, as we need to listen to the language and rhythms of the natural world as the path to the health and healing of the earth. Since the power to be affected and to affect, to be moved and move, a capacity which is indestructible, exhausted only with death, is constitutive of the body, there is an immanent politics residing in it: the capacity to transform itself, others, and change the world.

Silvia Federici

is a feminist activist, teacher and writer. Her published works include: Revolution at Point Zero. Housework, Reproduction, and Feminist Struggle (2012); Caliban and the Witch: Women, the Body and Primitive Accumulation (2004); Enduring Western Civilization: The Construction of Western Civilization and its "Others" (1994 editor).

Our Bodies Are Not Machines

My Resistance Will Be Bloody

(Niki Whiting)

I am thirteen and bleeding all over the floor of Renee's bathroom. It is the middle of the night. I thought I had to pee, but it's just that my period has started. I can't predict these unpredictable occurrences. My stomach hurts. I feel queasy. But my flow is so heavy it's running down my leg and making a mess on the floor. I mop up what I can. I swallow my pride and wake my friend to wake her mother. We need assistance. Thankfully, in an act of female teenage solidarity, no one ever hears of this story. Until now.

I am fifteen, crawling on my hands and knees through the halls of my high school. I have cramps so severe I cannot walk. I am pale and my English teacher is concerned that I might be passing out at my desk. Thankfully, most everyone is in class, so few people have to see my humiliation. But humiliation is the least of my concerns right now. Basic bodily functioning is my only priority at this moment. No one ever mentions seeing me do this.

I am nineteen and even being on the pill can't cure me of cramps so bad that once again I cannot walk. I am slumped on the tile floor of the university dining hall bathroom. I might be passing out. A male friend is brought in to find me and carry me back to my dorm room. He never mentions this again.

In each of these moments what isn't mentioned is that these moments aren't mentioned. Women are supposed to be quiet about something that our bodies do *every single month for thirty or forty years*. Don't make a big deal of your experience. Don't gross anyone out. This is shameful and people will mock you. Or they willfully ignore it.

Don't smell of flesh and blood. Don't leak or leave a bloody stain. Stuff your cunt up. Eat ungodly amounts of pain-killers. Alter your hormones with birth control pills, regardless of the sex you may or may not be having. Don't let cramps get you down; girl, let's see that smile! Don't rest; taking a day off work just proves women are weak and unreliable.

Patriarchy and Capitalism are cozy bedfellows. They are happy to convince women that their bodies are disgusting, so they can sell us one more product to make us more "productive", to make my vagina smell like candy or flowers, anything that will stop these cunts from bleeding.

HARDER STRONGER FASTER MORE

Anti-Capitalist efforts have always maintained the dignity of the human person, that our dignity is inherent in our being, and is not more nor less dignified according to our material wealth. Our bodies are not machines, and therefore we cannot work 12, 16, 18 hours a day. Thanks to the Socialists of the past, we now have an 8 hour work day.

Except, we don't really. Our paid work may only be 8 hours a day, but there is no room for rest in our society. In 1974 Silvia Federici tackled the issue of the unpaid work of housework, done almost exclusively by women. She says *"the unwaged condition of housework has been the most powerful weapon in reinforcing the common assumption that housework is not work, thus preventing women from struggling against it.[83]"* By denying that housework is work, that raising children is work, Capitalism can ignore women's needs for equality of time, reimbursement, and support. If it's not work, we can continue to underpay house cleaners, nannies, preschool teachers, (some) cooks, and so on.

We are encouraged to work ever longer hours. We are isolated in our nuclear families, not sharing the collective labor our lives require. Our communities are designed for long commutes. You can sleep when you're dead. Play hard. Never give up. Always improving, never just being. There is no room for pain, or rest, or love, but our bodies are not machines.

"Women's work," women's bodies, women's *embodied experience*, in fact, all human embodied experiences, are inconvenient for the Capitalist enterprise. Because our bodies are not machines.

> *"Women's work," women's bodies, women's embodied experience, in fact, all human embodied experiences, are inconvenient for the Capitalist enterprise.*

EMBRACING MY BLOODY BODY

In my late 20s, when I was in graduate school, I decided to try an experiment, because I could, because I had the flexibility to do so. I decided to give myself a 48 hour menstrual holiday. I was on the pill and could ensure that my period always started on a Friday. I would not make any plans. No studying if I could help it. I hung out in my pajamas, eating cheese burgers, napping, and watching Buffy the Vampire Slayer. And bleeding onto cloth. No pushing myself to look good (when I was bloated and heavily bleeding). No trying to socialize (when I was spacey and queasy). No needing to be ON. No bleached cotton and chemicals blocking me up.

It transformed the way I felt about my period and my body. I stopped hurting as much. I stopped experiencing PMS symptoms as strongly. I started looking forward to my body releasing and resting. I started wondering how many other people, particularly women, were pushing through pain and discomfort, ignoring their bodies, menstruating or not.

It changed the way I understood bodies, period. My compassion for others' bodies increased.

BY BEING SOFT I WILL RESIST

These days I don't have "days off." I have small children, born of a body so used to pain that labor was not that much worse than my cramps. When I am menstruating, I continue to observe my monthly holidays. I try not to schedule anything. We eat leftovers. I put my feet up. I embrace the blood that keeps my womb clean and healthy. I settle into a space, mentally, physically, and spiritually, that feels liminal and helps me wander between the realms of life and death, of this world and Other worlds.

By resting and embracing my bleeding I resist the fetishization of my female body. I don't have to smell like a prepubescent female. I can smell like the animal I am, iron and flesh, pheromones and earth. I listen to the completely natural urges of my body. Sometimes the slickness and warmth sing a song of sex, needing salt and a firm hand. Other times I want not a single touch, as if every inch of my flesh has gone on strike.

Instead of purchasing conventional period products, I have acquired, over time, cloth products, made by women who work out of their home. They are more environmentally sustainable, easily washable, more comfortable, and supporting, not some corporation, but a family and/or independent

---

craftsperson[84]. I step outside the conventional model and resist – economically, environmentally, bodily. One act of resistance leads to another.

BLOODY WILL BE THE WAY

I resist Capitalism by not being "productive." I resist by refusing to accept that my body or your body is a machine. Our bodies need to rest. Our bodies need time and space to heal, to purge, to grow, to be. Honoring my body shows my kids that the female body is not disgusting, but a cause for celebration.

Blood is life. The blood that pumps in my body and your body every moment of every day is life. Your heart's blood and my cunt's blood. A bleeding woman is a powerful woman. A bleeding woman can grow a life in the hidden spaces of her body. A woman who resists hiding her power, in her sex, in her blood, lays bare her connection to the sacrality of life, of our flesh.

Who better to understand this than Pagans? We understand the balance on the knife's edge between life and death. We understand that life is sacred, that blood and sex are sacred. The Capitalist system denies this sacredness and tries to shame us, male and female alike, by insisting that we soldier on, cover up, and purchase more goods to Get Through.

The body is a site of resistance. Resistance to Capitalism and Patriarchy may begin with a glimmer of a theoretical idea, realization, or hope. But those ideas must flower in relation to our lived, embodied experience. Resistance begins in these personal moments, in the ways we love, the ways we bleed, the ways we live and die.

I saw the tentacles of control between the two-headed hydra of Patriarchy and Capitalism, passing our bodies around. I cut one tentacle, only to see that we are tangled in others. But the confidence to cut one tentacle leads to cutting more. Resist once and you can resist again.

Resist beautifully. Bleed.

Niki Whiting

overthinks everything. She wears many hats, often simultaneously: parent, writer, student, witch, devotee, friend, singer. She likes her theory with a side of application, her theology wrapped in mysticism, and her old fashioneds made with rye.

---

84   Ironically, this form of resistance has finally been noticed by Capitalist powers and the FDA has decided that cloth pads are "class 1 medical devices" and must beregulated and taxed accordingly

Life Support Systems
(Fjothr Lokakvan)

Many things in the world today seem very dire: species are going extinct, ecosystems are being ruined, humans are waging wars and oppressing each other; all across the globe are signs that the state of the world, everywhere, is terrible.

There are those who look at these events and say that, as our life systems continue to collapse and take our civilizations and other beings with them, now is a time to treat the world as if it has gone into hospice, as if not only our death as a species is certain in the relatively near future, but the rest of the world's living systems as well.

It is true that things like global warming and its massive side effects will get worse before they can get better (we have not cut global carbon emissions enough yet); many species on the edge of extinction will cross over. Many ecosystems will be changed significantly—permanently, from our human-life-span perspective—into something different from what we have known for centuries.

But we do not have to react to this by falling into despair and hopelessness. And we do not have to tend only to the dead and dying, or to treat every living thing as if our primary concern is to help it pass on.

We can also use our magic, our devotion, and our relationships with spirit allies to help mend the holes in these damaged webs of relationships as best we can, to restore function and resilience.

If magic is making manifest your will in the world, then realizing (in the sense of causing something to become real) positive change —the conditions for further growth and the supporting of life—is a magical act with the intent to *keep this going*. It is to not let it be crushed by capitalism or kyriarchy or corporate greed, to defy and deny the people and processes that will destroy the life processes of the world, to say through action, "This world you create, dominators, shall not come to pass, it *is not* coming to pass. Another world *is* possible; I make it so."

Life *will* go on. In abundance and beauty and joyousness.

We must honor and mourn the dead—species, ecosystems small and large, cities, ways of life—giving special care to those brought to wrongful ends by the dominant culture. But we must also build resilience, for us now and for those who will remain after our deaths, that we-and-they can better come through the harder times yet to come. This will take time, it will take care, it will take hard work—but this is a process of love, it is love-in-action, and of hope, and it can be very joyful, as it affirms the value and delight and small triumphs of life where it would otherwise be put down by the obliterators.

Building stronger networks provides not only hope and support for the future, it is an act of resistance against the forces behind our worst current problems. Working together, creating commons, valuing life for itself—these things are antithetical to capitalism, imperialism, to all forms of abuse and power-over that harm human beings and the other beings and life systems we are entangled with.

Resilience is strengthened through reciprocity, maintaining healthy networks of relationships in which members support each other (not necessarily directly: things can be passed on, or through, one member to another). Reciprocity can be viewed as a form of love-in-action—it does not require strong affection for other members of the network, but a desire for the overall network to live and thrive. Doing something beneficial for a person or a river is expressing hope they will benefit from it – and perhaps in turn pass good actions along to others, or back to you, as a consequence of having benefited themselves.

Wild systems (aka "natural" systems) function this way, though it does not appear to be intentional the way human cultural networks have intention built into traditions of gift-giving, mutual aid, reciprocity, etc. The members of a wild ecosystem support and feed each other, and the outcome of these processes, over millennia, has been an ever-expanding diversity of life forms, in configurations that, barring major geological events, tend to be fairly stable for centuries or more. But remove a part of the network, whether it is a plant

or an apex consumer like a wolf, or dam a river, and the network becomes less stable, less resilient, more likely to change into a significantly different ecosystem. Some losses cause quick changes throughout the ecosystem; other changes take decades to become apparent. And sometimes a vanished species has its niche filled by another member of the system, but the biodiversity cannot be replaced without many, many more generations of evolution.

The dominant and dominating culture would flatten—is flattening—diversity, both biological and cultural. Anything that cannot be bent to feed capitalism and the kyriarchy is a threat to it, and has been ignored or attacked with intent to be destroyed. This flattening of diversity is the opposite of what life itself will do and has done for millions and millions of years.

We resist the dominant, dominating culture and its processes of obliteration of life's great diversities by reaffirming the value of life and by supporting life-supporting processes to encourage greater diversity. Among our means of resistance are love and joy and hope.

Love, to act with love, to love as an act, is to direct your energy to the betterment of the recipient of your love (self or other), not to confine or limit, but to encourage growth.

Joy is to find delight in the other, in yourself, in existence, in whatever is here before you and with you right now.

Hope is to see, based on more than wishful thinking, that better is possible and achievable, and to create a way forward.

LOVE

Love is tricky. Love is an emotion but it is also a verb—to love someone is not just a type of affection, it is to act towards them, or with them, in a way that may not have any connection with how affectionate you feel towards them. It is to treat them with care, with respect, with a sincere desire for their well-being and desires. It is not to seek to dominate them against their will.

To love in this way, to take care with someone (self or other) and work with or for them for their betterment, is to break with the dominant culture and its reinforcement of the "rightness" of dominating and looking for power-over, to be the "victor" in situations defined to only be perceivable as win-lose. To love does not necessarily mean everyone lives together happily ever after with each other —leaving a harmful situation is being loving to yourself; loving a group or place can require setting boundaries and keeping harmful influences out.

Capitalism, having perverted commerce with its approach of power-over, of power through accumulation of material goods (or symbolic representations of same), both monetizes and weaponizes love.

It preys upon normal human feelings, like the need for reciprocation of feelings, signs of affection, jealousy, feeling like you fit in with others, and so on, and repackages them as symptoms in need of quick fixes, rather than processes we need to come to terms with in a more functional way. Romantic love, long held to be a limited resource (one of the few resources the system believes IS finite! O the irony), is particularly targeted: the way to get it and hold onto it is to buy these things for your beloved to "prove" how much you care, so they won't leave you.

In or outside of romantic partnerships, if you aren't gaining enough under capitalism's influence to be able to buy the latest trendy object, then you're a moral failure, how can you face the rest of the social group without the newest widget? And what will you talk about?? (If you have the means to participate, but choose not to, then you're another kind of outcast.)

Capitalism also perverts the practice of reciprocity by making gift-giving an excessive obligation that many people do not feel a need to be on the receiving end of, but feel forced into participating in and *nobody is happy but the profit-counters*; it creates social pressure through marketing techniques, not to help support a healthy social network based on the members' and group's true needs or desires or best possible outcomes—but to benefit the producers of the most popular trendy items. Things that will, of course, "need" to be replaced in a year or maybe five; they are made that way. Holidays that are theoretically about family, about strengthening social bonds, *things that cannot be bought and sold*, have been overtaken to focus on the things bought and sold instead of the people. The few federally-recognized days off in the United States are not days off for retail workers, because these "breaks" from work have become "special sale" days, shopping days, encouraging people to save money rather than go somewhere to relax or see friends.

Exchanges of gifts can be beautiful, wonderful things; this is a legitimate way to act in a loving way towards someone. Thoughtfully done, in the right proportion to the relationship, understanding what is really needed or wanted, it helps strengthen human relationships and networks.

Gift-giving, whether material objects or gifts of time and attention, also strengthens relationships between us and the non-human beings we interact with through devotional practices, devotion being love and love-in-action. We are not alone in this world, and by strengthening our relationships with our Neighbors, we strengthen all parts of our

Capitalism, having perverted commerce with its approach of power-over, of power through accumulation of material goods (or symbolic representations of same), both monetizes and weaponizes love.

ecosystems, the human-made as well as the wild and the Other.

Joy

Joy is another form of resistance against the dominant culture, and a vital part of creating resilience to what that culture does to us.

I was depressed for several years, and it was nearly impossible during that time to find anything that brought me more than a temporary bit of joy; it was hard to even remember what that feeling was like previously. While the worst is gone, I know I'm not always that far from the edge of that pit, and some things make the ground tilt towards it. In addition, I have a bad habit of seeing something bad, or potentially bad, and working it up in my head into something that will be absolutely terribly awful, and then there's the ground pitching towards the void again.

I am pretty sure this is one of the reasons that, when I've been in distress and sought advice for how to handle the situation, the People Upstairs have advised me to focus on things I have in my life *right now* that bring me joy. It has been a good way to keep away from ground-tilting thoughts, or to pull away from them. It doesn't directly solve any problems, but it keeps me from over-focusing on my distress and fears, and gives me a greater ability to act on the problems.

I've also found the concept of joy an important, powerful thing outside of my personal life. It can be a transgressive act.

In Doris Lessing's *Prisons We Choose to Live Inside*, she writes,

> "The researchers of brainwashing and indoctrination discovered that people who knew how to laugh resisted best. The Turks, for instance ... the soldiers who faced their torturers with laughter sometimes survived when others did not. Fanatics don't laugh at themselves; laughter is by definition heretical, unless used cruelly, turned outwards against an opponent or enemy."[85]

And in an article on openDemocracy by Michael Edwards, about Sister Megan Rice (serving time in jail for breaking into a nuclear weapons plant to protest), he states,

> "In the face of bureaucratic authority, the expression

Joy is another form of resistance against the dominant culture, and a vital part of creating resilience to what that culture does to us.

of joy can be both powerful and subversive, partly because it is so unexpected. It disarms those in power through an absolute refusal to be provoked or humbled, and it provides great inner strength for the struggles that lie ahead."[86]

In the broader culture I am familiar with, expressing joy doesn't really seem to be encouraged (my cultural context is a white American from a basically WASP background). Acting "positive" is, of course, but spontaneous expressions of delight—not so much, though you're probably okay expressing delight about something among like-minded enthusiasts or friends. But generally, it really isn't the mature adult thing to do much of, is it? Unless you present it just right, dress it up in the right toned-down language, so it shows you know how to present emotions in a socially-acceptable manner. In addition, there's a nasty strain running through the culture that says if you're enjoying something, you're doing something wrong, not working hard enough, or you're merely getting your earned time away from "real life." Because real life isn't supposed to be enjoyable, I guess, unless you earn your pleasure through drudgery or pain first.[87]

I've seen similar things come up from time to time in discussions of pagan/polytheist practices, since they are embedded within this same context. A lot of people believe that, if you write too much about being happy about what's going on in your spiritual life, someone will "helpfully" point out to you that this is hard, and it is supposed to be hard and unpleasant. There's often a sense of an implied "Why aren't you suffering or struggling more?" and outright statements that if you don't find the hard painful parts in your spiritual practices, then you're not getting deep enough into your practice, you won't get out of it what you ought to, you won't ever really understand your gods, and so on. As in other parts of life, you risk being met with all kinds of skepticism, nonconstructive criticism, and outright scorn if you express happiness without also describing enough of the right kind of "hard work" and experience of pain.

---

85 Doris Lessing, Prisons We Choose to Live Inside, Harper and Row, Publishers, Inc., 1987

86 Michael Edwards, "To remain in prison for the rest of my life is the greatest honor you could give me: the story of Sister Megan Rice," openDemocracy.net, 2014

87 Why there is this notion that pleasure must be earned instead of being a birthright is another good question.

Of course it is important to understand that life, work, spiritual practices, relationships, etc., will have their ups and downs, and what those might look like in order to be prepared, but the kindest thing I can say to the people who feel obligated to respond to an expression of joy by squashing it is, "Please shut up. Come back later, in a different context, with your helpful advice about how things can be hard."

Listen: Joy is life affirming.

Lots of things in life hurt and suck. People know this. It is thoughtless if not cruel to respond to expressions of joy—or hope, or love, or other expressions of optimism—with what amounts to the message, "It is wrong for you to feel that, and to make sure you understand it's wrong to feel that, I'm going to hurt you for admitting you feel that way." Everyone must toe the cultural party line, or be brought to heel, attacked until forced into the right order.

The dominant culture, the kyriarchy, all the -isms that keep people down, they tell you/us: "You are wrong for being [that], and you are most definitely wrong for feeling joy or pride in being [that] or doing those stereotype-denying things. By the way, you'll also get put down for enjoying the things associated with the stereotypes." And so finding joy in life while being [that], in being alive as you are, defining for yourself who you are and what you enjoy, refutes the dominant culture and its abuses—and make no mistake, it is abusive to tell someone, "You are wrong to feel that way."

The ability to again feel simple joy-at-living, joy in what existed around me, was one of the first gifts I received after converting, and I find it precious beyond words. I thought I had lost that. Around the time I converted, I had gotten out of the worst depression—I felt real motivation and positivity for my future—but I still had no idea how to find that spark, that particular kind of easy delight-of-being again. Finding small moments of joy, reaffirming the goodness in life, now feels so much more important as a result. This excerpt from Mary Oliver's poem "Wild Geese" expresses something about this:

> "You do not have to be good.
> You do not have to walk on your knees
> For a hundred miles through the desert, repenting.
> You only have to let the soft animal of your body love

what it loves"

Take pleasure in simple comforts that come from being alive, whether it is good food, a soft place to rest, or the enjoyment of the wind, ocean, trees, or company of others. The basic things around us, things that are part of all animal live—if there isn't joy to be found here, among the circumstances in which we evolved, then where? How could an animal evolved to live surrounded by these phenomena not find some of them comforting and enjoyable? And how could finding joy in these things be wrong?

Oliver's poem concludes:

> "Whoever you are, no matter how lonely
> the world offers itself to your imagination,
> calls to you like the wild geese, harsh and exciting –
> over and over announcing your place
> in the family of things. "

There are so many amazing things in the world, all around us, all the time, and acknowledging that awesomeness acknowledges their value for simply existing.

Joy is life affirming.

We are surrounded by so many life-denying forces.

Joy is an antidote to their poisons and a reminder that there is more to existence than what they offer.

HOPE

The kind of hope that is wishful thinking is needed to get started—without a desire of some kind, there will be no action—but there is also a kind of hope that is based on seeing proof that things like that which is desired are possible. This provides encouragement to try other things, and a necessary reminder that not all is lost.

We create hope by resisting the dominant culture, by unlearning its lessons of power-over and learning instead what power-with means, and manifesting that in the world. Any change made to undo caused-harm is an act of hope, of enacting hope

We create hope by resisting the dominant culture, by unlearning its lessons of power-over and learning instead what power-with means, and manifesting that in the world. Any change made to undo caused-harm is an act of hope, of enacting hope: "another world IS possible, I-and-we make it so, one action at a time. There can be—there will be—more like this."

It took decades for industrial, fossil fuel-based culture to create terrible climate problems; it will take a long time to correct the problems, to help heal acres upon acres of strip-mined or chemically-soaked land, to address harms done to colonized peoples and places. To hope under these circumstances is sometimes to take many, many small steps towards something that will not see large results for decades. But this progress also provides hope for others working elsewhere—and some things can change dramatically for the better in a very short time. The Elwha River was dammed for over 100 years, but within a year of the dams' removal (which came after many decades of political effort), salmon returned, and long-absent sandbars and beach area are returning to the river's mouth, recreating tidal ecosystems. Many wild systems have a great deal of resilience inherent in them, and will eagerly return to pre-industrial states. Some will need much more, or ongoing, human effort.

Take encouragement from what others have done and are doing—and show others what can be done; mend the holes in the networks that they will be stronger when damaging forces contact them again. Do not focus too much on the harms being done—also find sources that tell you about the healing work, reminders that a better world is being made, and you are not alone. Look to those stories to help find your own way forward and to find other people to work with. Strengthen bonds through reciprocity and loving action, thus creating resilience in your human communities, in your places, and in your own life.

While this work of love and creating hope now and for the future is about webs of relationships, it is vital to not neglect yourself in all this. You are also part of many webs. Love yourself, hope for yourself (find it, make it), find joy in your circumstances.

That does not mean putting aside the harder things: If you need to grieve, grieve. Express your anger at what has been done. We aren't "supposed to" acknowledge "negative" feelings, either, if they are feelings about things the dominant culture has done, or what it tells us isn't valuable—wild things, people of the wrong skin color or gender presentation, the ability to find self-worth outside of a "real" job, etc. If we DID really feel those things, and even worse, talk to too many people about it, that would be a threat to the dominator culture—we might start understanding more how desperately it needs to be replaced with something healthier. Really allowing yourself to acknowledge and feel what you really feel, without bottling it up, making excuses, or putting it down is resistance. It is resistance to being silenced, resistance to falling quietly and obediently into the power structure, and it can help you become more resilient as well. If you have a handle on your feelings, they will have less power over you, and this is a great act of loving yourself.

Acts of resistance to the dominant, dominating culture that is behind the damage to our living systems and to our diverse cultural heritages are acts of love and of hope. And in the face of this damage we can—and must—look to where joy exists, to support us in this work, to remind us what it's all for.•

Fjothr Lokakvan

is an environmentalist, Lokean, and bioregional animist in Portland, Oregon, in Cascadia, with a great many Norse Giants and local Powers in her life. Her spiritual practices are focused on her relationship with her primary god and building relationships with the local Powers and place. She keeps houseplants, spends almost too much time on Tumblr, and is inordinately fond of birds. She regularly shares stories of ecological hope on the Gods & Radicals website and writes various and sundry other things at fjothr.wordpress.com.

The Dare
(Mandrake)

The world that has been lulled into a long, restless, uneasy sleep: I dare you to wake up. I dare you to stretch and sigh and wipe the sleep from your eyes and to look, really look at what's around you. I dare you to own your little place in this great big world – smaller now than it was before, yet staggering in its complexity. Look at where your life touches the lives around you, the seemingly insignificant and the apparently vital. Look at the sources of your power and how you use it, how you throw it away. Look at the big picture and at the microscopic details. Look.

Perhaps you were born asleep. Perhaps you've never once peered out the window toward the distant horizon, the beckoning darkness of the forested path. I dare you to open not only your eyes, but also your mind, and to question: what is real? What has value? What is necessary? What is better shared than owned? I dare you to wake from your wild, impossible dreams and to let yourself consider that your unarticulated desires are the map to a world worth waking up to.

Perhaps you have always been alone, isolated in the room where you sleep, desperate for a warm body beside you as nightmares steal your peace. Perhaps, worse, you have known hands that were raised in cruelty rather than affection. Perhaps you are afraid. And still, I dare you: open your heart to the possibility that we are a people whose continued existence depends urgently upon our ability to connect, deeply, to what is real in ourselves, to one another, and to the world of nature around us. I dare you to channel the bees, the ants, the geese, the starlings, to channel all those forces of nature that move instinctively as one. I dare you to feel the truth within you. I dare you to accept what you do not understand, to learn from what is foreign, to reach out and take hold of those whose hearts burn with the same fire as yours, no matter how unfamiliar.

the needs of another and to rush to meet them. I dare you to think in terms of we, of ours, and to seek the unique satisfaction that comes from giving to one who can give nothing in return. I dare you to turn away from the conventional notions of work and reward, to imagine new ways of living and being that are permeated with goodness that can't be profited by, only enjoyed.

Listen: the world is speaking. The voice may be that of the Gods, or of Nature herself, or that of the neighbor next door. Where are you being called? Where are you being dared to wake up, to turn away from what you think you are, what you think you know, what you are convinced you are here to do in this moment?

Perhaps you have only ever worked for your own survival, for that of your closest beloveds. Perhaps the world to you is a gaping maw threatening to swallow you whole. Perhaps you walk the razor's edge of dwindling hope for the future and fear of being unable to meet the demands of this moment. Perhaps you have wanted for nothing in your life.

Perhaps you have had all of your needs anticipated and met before you realize the need exists. Perhaps you've never thought to give without receiving something of equal value. I dare you to open your hands, to let your clinging cease, to share what keeps you bound and clenched. I dare you to see

I dare you: surprise yourself. Open your eyes. Open your heart. Open your hands. Even if you have always been silenced by your fear of the sound of your own voice, open your mouth and speak your truth. Become an example. Explore a world where community and independence weave and dance, where needs are met effortlessly, where fear is reserved for nightmares instead of life circumstances, other people, the wilderness inside.

Listen: I dare you to be changed.

Wake up.

Mandrake

is a High Priestess and Witch in the NorthStar tradition of Wicca, and a member of Baltimore Reclaiming. When she isn't in the kitchen or stained glass studio, you will find her playing outside in the urban wilderness, puttering in the garden, talking with the tarot, or writing, of course. Her blog can be found at http://theluckystone.co

The End and Everything After

Making Mars A Woman
(Sajia Sultana)

This world – we came here in vitro –
Cold and dry as a coelacanth fossil,
Yet red with blood's pigment.
In this land of winter we search for ice and snow
To force these deserts to flower
– to make this man our mother.

We search for the fossils
Of those we would supplant; maybe a trace of pigment,
Yeti tracks on Olympus snows –
Something that might be the ancestor of a flower –
Proof that this man was once a mother –
Could life be brought back in vitro ?

We paint this world with other pigments –
Blacken with mine-dust the crystalline snow.
Dig up cliffsides to plant foreign flowers.
Talk on the net to our abandoned mothers.
So many of us could only conceive in vitro,
Others leave behind space-suit fossils.

The heat of our reactors melts the salt-white snow,
Yet not enough heat to open wide these flowers –
So cold my hand, trying to mother
Germ-plasm of fauna and flora in vitro.
Wonder if our grandchildren's grandchildren will make fossil
Imprints on a landscape where we've muddied up the pigments.

Radiation wilted the first surface flowers.
This is not a safe world for children; still mothers
Sing of hope from outposts in vitro.
Hope that finds order in fossils,
A hope of order in mingled and separated pigments,
A hope as bright as the fading snow.

I have looked for a way for this soil to feed mothers,
For our lives to emerge from in vitro.
To shatter without shame the dust of fossils,
Prism rust into a million variable pigments.
To bring out edelweiss from beneath the virgin snow –
Touch carelessly that second flower.

Sajia Sultana

Sajia Sultana is a dancing songwriter living in Vancouver, Canada. She has released two albums, Bengali Winter and Girl,on sajiasultana.bandcamp.com. She is currently recording her third album and has a youtube channel showcasing her experiments in poetry and dance and the odd beauty tutorial at youtube.com/c/sajisultana

A Treatise On The Old Powers

(Max Oanad)

If you can read this, then we have something in common. We both come from the old time, before the catabolism, an event you might remember in old terms; market values, mechanical malfunctions, magnetic poles, solar storms, tectonic plates. We both remember watching as the cosmos refused those terms, shaking them off like broken shackles, running wild. We remember realizing the time we lived in was no longer ours. We realized that the bindings we had been trained to wield now only held us back, the universe we had been disciplined and trained to wield had broken free, leaving us ill-adapted to the semiologies of survival emerging around us.

We watched our younger siblings, who never expected anything else, take to the feral cosmos with an unfearing proficiency. Using tools we often cannot perceive properly, they created a world in which we are increasingly anathema. All the while we watch dumbfounded, not old enough to have been heroes; Great Ones who shepherded whatever humans they could into this new time, but old enough so that our expectations of the old world haunt our ability to participate in this one. Like fish whose younger siblings crawl out of the water to breath the air and see the sky, we watch, unable to follow, unable to see past the surface, which for us is still the sky.

In the world we were trained for, being an adult meant knowing how to read, how to write, how to do math, how to drive a car, understanding how money worked, how time worked, how laws worked. In this world, such things would be frivolities if they were not so tedious. Not only are they useless, but they can endanger a growing mind which needs to learn other things, like how to use blood to awaken a bike and keep it alive, how to navigate an airship through the storms of lost thoughts, how to listen to the song of the stars and call water from the other three elements, how to see a horizon beast, and gain its trust. This is why we will always be outsiders, because we will never be able to do these things.

No doubt you have found this document as part of your search for those old powers which had once been our birthright, powers which could once bring all of existence to heel. Understand that I once wished to do the same thing.

When I was little, people would ask me what I wanted to be. I told them I wanted to be an astronaut. Such a fun, ambitious sounding word for what they used to call "a girl". It seems silly, antiquated and overcomplicated, now that all you need is someone who can sing the Song of Folding Distances to walk in the light of any sun you wish. Still, I can remember staring up at the sky as its meaning changed, as I realized the word astronaut would never make sense again.

I remember looking up words adults used to try to explain what was happening, applying images to names, as if the answer to saving everything lay in understanding what the adults were talking about. Eventually, the adults stopped having words for things. After that, the adults I knew were gone, and instead there was Pama Tu, a different kind of adult, the kind that I had been told not to stare at.

Somehow Pama Tu and the others like them knew how to live in this new time, and they showed us how as best they could. They taught us how to gather water from the air with screens and filter it in barrels of gravel, how to find food and how to make food more plentiful, how to hide while we waited for the last bullet to be fired, knowing that there would be no way to make more.

At some point, I understood what I had been frantically trying to stop had already happened, that the bound and subdued world which had been promised to me once I was old enough to wield it had escaped forever. What was left were so many broken pedestals in the desert, the names of which only I, and others like me, could read because our minds had already paid that terrible cost.

I had been reading for years when they discovered it made the difference between the old minds and the new, that it was almost as bad as coming to sentience inside a room full of right angles. I tried to stop reading, but the damage had been done. No strange unimaginable powers awakened within me, I could not perceive new patterns in nature, no ancient reawakened beings came to teach me their language and ways.

I can remember when many of the younger children started talking about strange animals we couldn't see which grazed on the ruins of the old world. They would be gone for days and return with stories too strange to believe until the day they took us to gather mint, wild onions, and tubers in places

that should have been only ruin and desolation. I can remember my mind straining to see beyond the lines I used to distinguish one thing from another, catching for a brief moment a glimpse of the new patterns drifting over the land and making it blossom, my younger siblings riding them like dancers on the horizon. I remember Pama Tu, standing there in bewilderment looking at me and saying "Who ever thought, back when I rode a subway to a building where I gave my life to nothing, that the world would shape up like this?"

I should have been happy, but I ran to Pama Tu and sobbed, "Why can't I see them? Why can't I ride them?" They comforted me as best they could, but they were as powerless as I in the face of this world and its indifferent wonders. I retreated to my books and my typewriter, hoping that words might be my power.

I quickly learned that the stagnancy of words was no longer useful in a place where things attached to other things and became something new altogether. Using the old words kept me from perceiving the chaos, a comfort that locked my mind into one state, one angle, one moment of a thing, and in doing so losing its emerging totality. In the old world, everything had already been categorized and decided in a way that the Great Ones said trapped their potential. When things freed themselves, resulting in the catabolism, when so many new things emerged, the Great Ones wanted to leave things as unsorted as they could, letting the children born to this world create the language they would use to swim in it.

As others like me, I struggled to understand the language they came up with, a language as free from rules and structures as the age which it gave meaning.

I remember rebelliously naming the place we lived the Fractured Planes/Plains, thinking it was clever that both words could be spoken at the same time. Now, the name is a joke. They will come up to me, point out at whatever comprises the landscape, and laughingly say the name that I gave it so long ago. What really gets them going is when I try to explain why it ever made sense in the first place.

Instead of giving up, I retreated even further into the written. I committed my mind to the impossible task of translating every ever-changing thing into the language of the old time. This they warily indulged, and I was often given pens, along with scavenged books and paper, the edges torn off to

In the old world, everything had already been categorized and decided in a way that the Great Ones said trapped their potential.

break the rectangles, thus mitigating the risk of invoking the baleful old powers.

One day Pama Tu, after noticing I'd been feverishly working at my writing for hours, came and sat next to me. We had discussed this kind of thing before, why I buried myself in words, my isolation, why I thought this was my only choice in the face of the unfairness of the world. But tonight something was different. Something about the way they spoke.

"I know that you don't remember much of the old world. Even though you've heard the stories, you can't know the way that words hunted us, the way that numbers waited for us at night. Our lives spent in rectangles as we worked in numbers and words. When I wasn't thinking of words and numbers, I was dreaming of some kind of different world, and when the chance for that world came—when the catabolism happened and we were able to see beyond the rectangles that had been drawn around us—I realized that chance had arrived. I won't pretend that I understand you, but when I see you working at this thing the way you do, I see someone who is waiting for their chance."

They gripped my hand and looked into my eyes. "When my chance came, I was ready to dance on these new winds, but I saw you and all these other little storm seeds and I knew I had to bring you with me just to see what you would grow into. I promise you that one day your chance will come, but every chance comes with a choice about how you will shape this world. So go back to your words, just don't forget that there is a world beyond them, a world that is worth protecting."

I had no idea what they were talking about. All I remembered from the old world was that it had been stable, it had been safe, and it had been mine. I had no idea of the ancient and compulsive horrors which had been used to break people like Pama Tu, which could be resummoned into the world. I had a faint recollection of things like ammunition, things like laws, things like debt; things which I could never fully understand. I knew how those words were defined by other words and how they made numbers change, but I didn't learn how those words and numbers changed the world, changed the heart –until they took Pama Tu.

We had grown up hearing stories about debt, about how the old world ran on its power to compel people to do things against their will. Like everyone, we were told never to expect to get back what we had given. To do such a thing would give us an unnatural power over the other person, that it would cause both people to think in numbers in harmful ways, making other things invisible or irrelevant.

We knew that Pama Tu, like all of the Great Ones, had debt. That was how things were before the catabolism, people had no choice about things, everything was built up so that everyone had to serve the old powers that ran on debt and spewed ammunition. Even the ones like Pama Tu, who could see them and fight against them, were still a part of them; they had debt and fired ammunition, or made it, or made things for the people who did. As Pama Tu liked to say "you either made ammunition, or you cleaned for the people who did".

In a world where people ride the beasts of the horizon, build airships and blood bikes and hear the songs of stars on water, the stories the Great Ones told about the world before the catabolism were just stories, stories to scare us off to bed or to keep us in line. Behave, or the ways of the old world will return. Even I, who spent my time reading about these things, and had the vaguest memories of them, had trouble imagining it.

And so when we heard the rumors of men riding on strange, loud machines, men who were tracking down and hunting the Great Ones for their debt, we were not nearly as afraid or angry as we should have been. After all, such a thing seemed too distant and strange to be real. We should have known better.

They took Pama Tu when they went into the new grazing grounds. We should have stopped them, but to be fair, they didn't believe any more than we did that the old powers would come back. They wanted to look at the sunlight on the old brick buildings just after the rain. They said that there was no sight quite like it, they wanted to see it before the beasts got to it, and really, who were we to stop them?

When the rain returned, but Pama Tu didn't, we worried. A group of listeners went into the grazing grounds to find them, returning with nothing except a story about the bricks and broken concrete, a story of a quiet moment in the sun after the rain, a story of that moment being broken by men in

We had grown up hearing stories about debt, about how the old world ran on its power to compel people to do things against their will.

heavy vehicles with chains and whips and dogs, men who barked like dogs, whose barks could still be heard alongside Pama Tu swearing and screaming for help ringing faintly in the glass of the broken windows. That is what they told me.

They sent riders to find out if others had lost Great Ones in this way, to invite them to a gathering so that we could find out what was happening and get our Great Ones back. The First People, whose knowledges went back to before the old world, whose ways of living had survived the destructive terror of the old powers even as they bore the brunt of their wrath, they also came to the gathering because their Elders had been taken.

It did not take us long to find the place where they had brought our Great Ones and the Elders of the First People. We went in the direction where the ash in the sky was coming from, we followed the waters which ran red with something that made the mouth and throat burn. The sky cried out where they were. As we moved forward under ever darkening skies and poisoned rivers, we heard the listeners tell us

what had happened when the Great Ones and the Elders and their kidnappers had passed this way: where the ancient machines had stopped, where people had tried to escape and how; where they had been recaptured, and how they had been punished.

When we arrived at the place where they had taken our Great Ones and the Elders, our heads were full of the listeners' stories. We could not mistake the sight of the place, so unmistakable, and it was almost too much to bear.

You can tell when the powers of the old world are being invoked because to do so involves using geometries that do not naturally occur on this plane. There is a shape that I can draw on a piece of paper, which to me looks like a three dimensional cube; to my younger siblings, it looks like so many surgical slices in the fabric of the universe, threatening to bind their minds.

The depiction of such a shape was terrifying enough for them, but the actual construction was something their minds, and what we people used to call sanity, was not capable of bearing. And so when we saw the place where they had taken our Great Ones and the Elders; this perfectly cubic wall, with so many smaller cubes inside, the relentlessly Euclidean geometries summoning forth the eldritch forces long dispelled from this world, imprisoning the people we loved as it leeched poison into the earth, into the sky and into waters, many of my siblings fell to the earth, gripping it desperately.

What we did not know is that the people who had taken our Great Ones were already expecting us. They sent men out to tell us that they understood why were upset, but that they had an explanation, and if some of us were to tour the place with them, we would come back and be able to explain everything to everyone else.

Of the entire horde assembled, I was the only in-between child. Even if any of my younger siblings were willing to enter that baleful plane, to walk with those who had summoned the old ways, they might not be able to see what needed to be seen, and navigate the laws of that place without becoming bound to them.

My hands shook as I stepped forward to volunteer. I had spent the better part of my life reminiscing and fantasizing about the old world. Yet there was a stark difference between my imaginings and this towering place. It was terrifyingly real, and yet I could still remember entire landscapes of such places stretching to the horizon before the catabolism. This place was nothing compared to the powers as they existed before, the powers which as a child I had not feared. I said this to myself as my knees buckled and my courage faltered in the face of this thing that threatened to devour everything I had known since I had been with Pama Tu.

Pama Tu! They were inside this place, them and others like them, so precious to us. Someone had to go in and see them, to find them, to see if they were alright, and how could they be alright in a place like this? So I stepped forward and said "I will go in with you. I will tell the others what I see."

I almost expected someone to speak out against me, to say that I couldn't be trusted, that I was an in-between child and so might be lured into the old ways. They would have been right. Even I didn't know if the very power of that place, and my mind's attunement to it, would be too powerful to resist. Instead, the ones who could muster the strength to walk over to me did.

They gathered around me, draping me with protections, some of which I could see and feel, others I could not. Some of them looked me in the eyes as they offered me voice gifts:

"May this one walk into the darkness untouched,"

"May the threads which connect this one to us remain unsevered,"

"May this one see with clarity past all illusions,"

"May this one return to us, whole as they are now."

Feeling the power of these gifts surrounding me and coursing through me, I turned to the men, and followed them to the entrance.

The gate opened, and I turned to look back one more time at the beauty of the great horde spread across a landscape that I still could not make sense of, but which had become home. Then I followed the men across the threshold, and entered the rectangle.

There was nothing the hordes could give me that would have protected me from the power of that place. The moment I stepped through the gate, the charms around my neck, arms, shoulders, head and waist became so many pointless gaudy baubles, the words they had spoken became pithy sayings in the face of a relentlessly stable Truth. Nothing coursed through me. Nothing connected me to anything. Naked in a world of right angles, I was home.

I had entered reality again. For the first time since the catabolism, everything around me made sense. It took a few seconds for my mind to readjust to the old forms, as if I had been on a boat since the catabolism, and had just stepped now back onto solid ground. For the first time since the catabolism, I could point at something and name it, and be right. I could name everything I was looking at: stairs, bars, locks, crates.

They had brought back things that I had thought were lost forever— how had they found them?

They had brought back things that I had thought were lost forever—how had they found them? I stared at the screens full of numbers and the papers full of numbers as the men explained to me how all of our Great Ones had debt which they had never been able to get rid of. But now these men had found a way to help them get rid of it, because they had also found how to make ammunition. By making ammunition, our Great Ones could get rid of their debt.

There it was. They had awakened the power of debt. They had harnessed it and used it to compel our Great Ones in this place. Suddenly they felt less great to me. The debt hung on them like a stain, something they had tried to hide, and Pama Tu had been good at hiding it. Maybe that was why they didn't want us to talk about it, that was why they were afraid of it, they knew that if we understood debt, we would see them for what they were. They were people who had taken and not given back. There it was, all in the numbers, in the words. You could measure their worth, the absence of their worth, the vacuum of their worth. A vacuum they could fill in this place and become whole again.

Then they took me to see the ones with debt, to watch them mixing powders, making shells and casings, filling those shells and casings with powder. I listened as the men explained how the Great Ones had lied to us all about the old world; in the old world people had things that until now we would never have, but now we had a chance to have those things again. There they were: the computers, the papers, the wires, the water that had been forced into the walls.

I looked at the ones with debt, the ones that were now workers, they were wretched. Their eyes were sad and empty as they gave the reawakened old powers what was owed. I tried to feel pity, but all I could feel was embarrassment for them. They had let themselves have debt, why should we trust them with anything? I wanted to help them, but I could feel the strength of the old powers and knew that this was just the way things were. I tried to find Pama Tu amongst them, and I may have seen them, or someone that looked like them, but everything looked different in this place.

They took me to another room, showed me more papers full of words and numbers, the ones which promised to release their workers if others agreed to work to fulfill their debts. Amidst the beeping and the clicking and the clanging, the men offered me perfectly rectangular papers which explained how many people the gathered horde needed to give the men and how many years would pass until more people would need to be brought to this place. I took the papers, feeling the power that they conferred. I held them as I was led back out to the threshold, back to the world that would never be home, the world that would never be something I could understand no matter how long I lived there. I crossed back to the horde and tried to remember that they had once been my people.

It was hard to make sense of anything. My memories of the catabolism were that it had been violent and sudden. I had not realized how gradual the transition from the old world to this one had been, until now, as my mind stepped instantly from the old reality to this one. I was unable to latch onto anything that would make everything else make sense. The landscape buckled, someone was screaming to music which made the people change colors. Worlds grew like grain and became stars on the clear water of a sun drenched ocean. Some of them were people, or animals.

I stood on that ocean. I tried to tune out the song, tried to navigate by memory, but everything had already escaped my memories, had become something else. My connection to this time had been severed. Whatever habits of mind I had used to translate this present into something I could understand had been lost when I had entered the rectangle.

I was sure they were all there, staring at me, waiting for me to tell them what I had seen, but how could I? What words would I use to describe the incomprehensible to the incomprehensible? Standing on the threshold between two worlds, neither of which I could fully translate to the other, I realized that this was what I had been waiting for. All that time keeping the words, understanding the old world—everything had been to prepare me for this moment, and yet I was not ready.

All I had was the knowledge that back inside the rectangle lay a place and a time in which I had power. My entire being wanted nothing more than to crawl back inside, to live there, to join the men as we brought the world to heel with the old powers. I would watch my siblings who had once mocked me made hollow and meaningless by toil.

This was what Pama Tu had meant about my choice, but it didn't really feel like a choice. Her words were the words of an indebted, who would have done anything, said anything, to not pay back what she owed the old powers. I had to find a way to explain to them what needed to happen, how many people they needed to send in, for how long, and how many more people after that. I stared at the sheets of paper, feeling their power, trying to find a way to bring that power into this place, this time beyond the catabolism.

What I had forgotten was that this time and this place, and the people who belonged here, had powers all their own. They did not care whether I could perceive them or believe in them, they surrounded me like a thick inconvenience, making it hard for me to make out the words on the sheets, making it hard for me to turn what I had to say into words that could be understood by the horde.

As I stood there, trying to find the words that would make my siblings bow to the powers of the old world, I flashed on a memory, a summer day when I had taken all of the ice out of the freezer to make a snow fort. I remembered the hand on my shoulder as I stared confused at the small pile of ice slumping in the sunlight, the dawning understanding that our cunning cannot always overcome the passage of time and the changing of the seasons.

There had been rumors about what had caused the catabolism, that this was just a great cosmic season that we had not yet understood, that it had been caused by a scientist, that it had been the only way to save the world from imminent destruction. Whatever the reasons, there had been reasons, and those reasons were greater than me and my need to live in a world that I could understand, where power could be something I could hold over others as had been my destiny in the old world.

I tore the pieces of paper apart. I refused to think or speak about what the men had said inside the walls of that terrible place. Instead, I turned, I pointed at the walls, the only stable thing in my field of vision, and I screamed. I screamed because I wanted that world back, I screamed because it scared me, but I also screamed because this was my moment, and I took it against all the temptation the old powers could offer me. I could not speak against them, but I could point and scream.

I screamed because I wanted that world back, I screamed because it scared me, but I also screamed because this was my moment, and I took it against all the temptation the old powers could offer me. I could not speak against them, but I could point and scream.

The air came rushing at my back, and then the horde began rushing past me like leaves on the wind, and then they were like the ocean, like the tide.

I watched men behind the walls invoke their munitions.

And then I saw, with terrible, relentless clarity. I saw the skyskippers diving between their airships, my beast-riding siblings, half naked blood-bike warriors, this-plane-that-plane dancers in their shawls and scarves, and others who will not let themselves be written about, bringing everything they had against the grey rectangle.

None of the horde, despite their numbers, had ever encountered ammunition before, let alone had its flesh-destroying power used against them. I had memories of ammunition, of seeing it being used before, but nothing could prepare me for what I witnessed on that day.

Entire bands were annihilated in single explosions, the bodies of people who were once loved and touched and who had destinies transformed in a flash into something too terrible to look upon. Airships fell from the sky, skyskippers tore apart screaming.

There are many things that I saw that day that I wish I could forget, but that day is a part of me. For all of the horrible things that happened, I am glad, because I witnessed the old powers at their most baleful, I watched them unleash their brutality against my siblings threatening time and future itself, and I watched that brutality fail in the face of the new wonders.

We did not leave any of the men who had summoned the old powers alive. Their blood and skulls were given to the blood-bike riders, who bound their souls to power their bikes. The papers full of numbers were burned, ashes scattered to the winds, the computers broken down and reconfigured by circuitwrights. The airships broke their walls into piles of rubble, and my siblings let their herds trample and graze the rubble until there were no stones. When we left that place nothing remained of the men or their work, except for the memorials to our dead, and the sprouting orchard which the herd had left in their wake.

Doubtless there are other writings and numbers which keep the debts of our Great Ones, and other writings and figures which tell how more such places could be built. I am sure that there are people out there who want to find these writings to bring back the old ways. Yet understanding such a thing would require someone to be able to read. This is why I have written this story down, because I wanted you to find it first.

If you can read this, then you are the enemy. You cannot see or know the world that that has come, and so you might be tempted to bring back the ways of the old world. Understand that we will give our last dying breath to stop you. We will give no warning, there will be no hesitating or negotiating, we will destroy you as we destroyed the others. This is your warning. The old powers cannot protect you.

Max Oanad

is a practicing pagan, teacher, writer and over-thinker living in Portland, Oregon, where he cultivates relationships with Celtic deities, local land spirits, and human beings.

The World Will Not End But We May Change (T. Thorn Coyle)

Awaken to the sounds of apocalypse:
Quiet house. Distant traffic.
Water boiling once the kettle is switched on.
The striking of a match.
The hiss of candle lighting.
And my prayers...

I am sure in other places
Apocalypse sounds different.

Children petulant from lack of food.
Fighting over money
or who gets to use the car,
Who takes the bus.
The concussion of a bomb
From silent skies.

Apocalypses don't come sudden.
They can sound like day to day.

We run after each other
Arms upraised to catch a falling world.
They keep telling us the sky
Is firm above,
But it is slippery as their lies,
That tell us nothing we don't know.

This world is ending.
Every sound announces so.

Some day we will waken to the sounds
Of a new world.
What will that sound like?
A woman rolling over to make love.
A kettle hissing. A match striking.
And a child eating his breakfast.

Beginning or ending,
The ordinary things are what we have.

T. Thorn Coyle

is a magic worker and Pagan committed to love, liberation, and justice. Thorn is the author of the novel Like Water and the collection of magical tales Alighting on His Shoulders. Her spiritual writing includes: Sigil Magic for Writers, Artists & Other Creatives; Make Magic of Your Life; Kissing the Limitless; Evolutionary Witchcraft; and Crafting a Daily Practice. Thorn works to build a society based on love, equity, justice, and beauty.

A Counter-Apocalypse For Our Time

An essay in six polemical theses
(Virgilio Rivas)

FIRST THESIS

Is there a counter-narrative to the apocalypse? And to whose apocalypse are we to offer a different story? Starting from the ancient Greeks who understood the apocalypse as the unveiling of what came before the start of a new era, the idea of the 'end' was bound to the notion of the uncanny. The past is unveiled by the apocalypse as in itself the trace of what preceded it, and so on.

If 'Greek' is considered the language of the apocalypse, it was a language used later in the Gospel in a very bad, creolized sense (Hebraic Greek), not to mention "sloppy and careless."[88] If we expand this interesting detail to a certain affirmation of dead traces, traces whose origins were already lost, then as the revelations of John were to give us the unmistakable example, "a creolization of the Greek dominant language with Semitic lexical and syntactical elements," as one scholar accordingly observes, "would have been a spoken language only"[89] which means no "literary traces" could ever attest to it.[90] The intrigue goes on:

> "The language of the apocalypse presents not the dialect of a subaltern community that has only imperfectly internalized the dominant language, but an idiolect, the peculiar language of one author, unattested anywhere else in antiquity.[91]"

This enigma of the idiolect will give us something to unveil in the next few pages.

---

88 See David L. Mathewson, *Verbal Aspect in the Book of Revelation: The Function of Greek Verb Tenses in John's Apocalypse* (Leiden, Boston: Brill, 2010), 2.

89 Allen Dwight Callahan, "The Language of the Apocalypse," *The Harvard Theological Review*, Vol. 88 4 (October 1995), 458.

90 Ibid

91 Ibid.

Second Thesis

What the apocalypse unveils of the past also contains a risk or a promise, like a *pharmakon* which cures but also acts on its desire to poison its host.[92] The apocalypse can endanger the security of the present whose very possibility rests on the quiet power of the uncanny, which it nonetheless denies; the vaguely familiar of which no amount of conception can come close to the understanding without breaking itself into pieces. Arguably, only a Buddhist has ever come close to this path.[93] How the apocalypse has transformed from its relatedness backward into something else entirely—that is, in the aheadness of one's ownmost potential,[94] it is a story that philosophy even today would refuse to tell. On top of it is the restriction against telling a story if one is to pursue the clearest path to the essence of things. Heidegger is a bit disappointing for us in this case: "Our first philosophical step consists in not...'telling a story'—that is to say, in not defining entities as entities by tracing them back in their origin to some other entities."[95] This is the classic conception of the triumph of logos over mythos, the victory of conception over storytelling which refers to philosophy's alleged break with the past.

With respect to its early beginnings, from the natural philosophers and right on up to Plato himself (that is, Plato without Platonism), philosophy emerged out of the ruins of the old world. But even that world refused to unveil its true origin. This counter-refusal is the uncanny's wayward causation: coming from behind the present's fantasizing about its self-image. We can witness in Aristotle how logical representation will end this errant causality, mistaking the logos for the true power that had borne it.

We can recall here Plato's dilemma, which consists in unveiling the origination of philosophy in its mythic past in a manner most distinctive of confronting the apocalypse, utilizing the past's enduring heritage, speaking of its unveiling technique, the narrative form. The narrative form is the foil

92   See Michael A. Rinella, *Pharmakon: Plato, Drug Culture, and Identity in Ancient Athens* (United Kingdom: Lexington Books, 2010).

93   See Mark Epstein, *Going to Pieces Without Falling Apart: A Buddhist Perspective on Wholeness* (New York: Broadway Books, 1999).

94   Martin Heidegger, *Being and Time*, trans. John Macquarrie and Edward Robinson (Oxford: Basil Blackwell, 1962), 28.

95   Ibid., 26.

in the consistency of the present. In fact, it withdraws from it by depriving the present of its relatedness to time in its attempt to extend indefinitely to the future. No wonder we have a present devoid of a sense of security, in the same manner the present suppresses what feeds on its insecurity. The present has always been attracted to the allure of the apocalypse, yet only by suppressing it does this attraction come into play.

Heidegger once thought of the future of this allure ceasing to be a kind of destiny that compels in the guise of overcoming metaphysics.[96] Can humanity "overcome" a destiny as compelling as the ontological difference, or rather, the historical necessity of the mutual opposition of beings and Being in the unfolding of their unity, courtesy of phenomenological hermeneutics? [97] If it is essential that an 'insufficient principle' be thrown away (as Kant cried out in the opening pages of the first *Critique* [98]), the principle, for our own purposes here, being 'Man' who can never come close to the understanding that his destiny in Being is a potential for change, we may want to raise a point of order in the following: can humanity overcome its destiny in which it is also necessary that it be transformed into something else, from the inquiring type to that of the storytelling? All these are questions of necessity, as we shall see.

Necessity, however, as the first philosophers understood it, is a type of causation that always errs; an errant throw of creation that the contemporary now calls by its name *hyperchaos*[99] whose secret it is said only a poem could unravel, but always leaves the uncanny. One can think of Mallarmé with his throw of the dice (coup de dés).[100] With the errancy of the

The present has always been attracted to the allure of the apocalypse, yet only by suppressing it does this attraction come into play.

throw the uncanny is unveiled of its secret, the secret being, among others, that the poet Mallarme "threw and did not throw," that Chance or contingency is, simply enough, a necessity.[101] This is the secret of the necessity of creation, an errant throw of chance. In the *Timaeus*, however, Plato would have us acknowledge this necessity by its true name, arguably, the first name, *chora*.[102]

The chora—this apocalyptic figure, an unattested idiolect—is neither being nor becoming. Being and becoming are reducible to the assertive logic of reason, whereas chora is beyond it or rather exceeds its grasp. Only by telling a story (through the monologue of *Timaeus*) can it be brought to the attention of listeners—listeners who had agreed beforehand that no amount of reason could explain what they agreed to hear about:the creation of the cosmos.

The chora is an outcome of storytelling, by all means unattested like the idiolect of the Hebraic-Greek. If the chora is the necessary precondition for the creation of the cosmos, out of which being and becoming would perform their respective duties, then only by telling a story can the cosmos emerge. Only by pursuing in narrative form the unravelling of the cosmos from its precondition, its bastard conception, an errant cause, can the whole process of creation begin. An anal type of creation, call it Deleuzian buggery,[103] is nonetheless too modern to comprehend a fundamental sense of perversity, though it has its own strength intended to rip apart all hitherto traditional forms of conceiving, engendering as much errancy as there are various words for delirium vis-à-vis the all-pervasive

96   Martin Heidegger, *The Question Concerning Technology and Other Essays*, trans, William Lovitt (New York and London: Garland Publishing, Inc., 1977), 26.

97   See Dominique Janicaud, *Heidegger from Metaphysics to Thought*, trans. Michael Gendre (Albany: State University of New York Press, 1995), 23.

98   We are alluding to Kant's statement in the Critique of Pure Reason: "In fact, pure reason is so perfect a unity that, if its principle were insufficient for the solution of even a single one of all the questions assigned to reason by its own nature, then we might just as well throw the principle away" (See Immanuel Kant, *Critique of Pure Reason*, trans. Werner Pluhar [Indianapolis and Cambridge: Hackett Publishing Company, Inc., 1996], 9).

99   See Quentin Meillassoux, *After Finitude. An Essay on the Necessity of Contingency*, trans. Brassier (London: Continuum, 2008), 58.

100   See Quentin Meillassoux, *The Number and the Siren. A Decipherment of Mallarmé's Coup de Dés*, trans. Robin Mackay (United Kingdom:

Urbanomic Press, 2012).

101   Ibid., 222.

102   See Plato, *Plato: Timaeus and Critias*, trans. Robin Waterfield. (Oxford: Oxford University Press, 2008). Recall that Aristotle rejected Plato's version of the chora in favor of another likely story, from Hesiod. In his Theogony, Hesiod proposed that in the beginning there was chaos ... and before there could be anything else there must be a room (chora) to be occupied" (line 117-118, in See Hesiod, Hesiod, "Theogony," in *The Homeric Hymns and Homerica*, trans. Hugh G. Evelyn-White, ed. G.P. Goold [Cambridge, Massachusetts: Harvard University Press, 1982], 87; lines 117-11]). Aristotle cited Hesiod to reject Plato's version which in Book IV of Physics received a new definition as place or topos of creation, effectively reducing the chora to being (See Aristotle, "Physics: Book IV," in *The Complete Works of Aristotle*, ed. Jonathan Barnes [Princeton, New Jersey: Princeton University Press, 1991], 51; 208b30).

103   See Gilles Deleuze and Claire Parnet, *Dialogues*, trans. Hugh Tomlinson (New York: Columbia University Press, 1987).

claim to certainty. Certainty traces its own work to the dynamics of desire but for some reasons suppresses it. But in lieu of anal perversity, chora, the bastard concept, is rather originally the outcome of incest, between man and his virginal Mother.[104] And since a story is irreducible to reason, irreducible either to being or becoming, the perverse itself is resistant to finality, the finality of causation.

But when desire is consummated through the intervention of a positive power greater than it,[105] or rather, in this surrender of infinite horizontal vitality to the absolute measure of finitude (with its vertical hierarchy of beings and entities), we cannot for a moment doubt that Hiroshima and Nagasaki were already achieved in Athens. This thought that final causation could replace the horizontal infinity of life was realized by laying plunder to the city, and the war against the uncanny is at the heart of this causation.

> *We cannot for a moment doubt that Hiroshima and Nagasaki were already achieved in Athens. This thought that final causation could replace the horizontal infinity of life was realized by laying plunder to the city, and the war against the uncanny is at the heart of this causation*

Right on it was also the beginning of ultimate pornography where everything must submit to presence. Aristostle unrolled the Greek terms to represent this new idiolect of enlightenment, *logos apophantikos*. Aristostle's great patron in Nazi Germany, Heidegger, least suspected he was offering the same pornography as bradnsiehd by his mentor—the "splendour of radiant appearing."[106] The advent of logical representation thus put an end to the Grecian apocalypse. This came as the great moment of liberation of thinking from the uncanny, as we can deduce from the invention of causes.

THIRD THESIS

Here, we are being led to confront a new apocalypse. But it may be well to note an important intervening principle.

Influenced by Paul's Letter to the Thessalonians, Carl Schmitt earlier introduced the idea of suppressing the apocalypse in the guise of creating the necessary conditions for peace.[107] The *katechon*—something or someone who has already seen the end of time—will suppress the apocalypse. It would appear though that peace is essential not only to suppress the apocalypse but the errant causation of the uncanny as well. The fear that the uncanny may resurface, despite the blockade, is not improbable. As Derrida once asked, is not the uncanny "the great problematic constellation of haunting"?[108] The uncanny has a distinct relation to necessity, and here necessity approximates the degree to which Derrida describes ontology as hauntology or "the return of the repressed," in which the spectral takes precedence over being [or] existence."[109]

But peace, what is it? How does it reveal the uncanny?

Each time a war is concluded, an uncanny moment resurfaces. As a genuine ally of war, peace is tasked with the curious responsibility to bring survivors to bear the authentic experience of apocalypse. Survivors alone suffer the full extent of war and only in the time of peace, when war leaves traces of time withdrawing from the present. Peace deepens the ugliness of war. War is to attain peace as peace is to sustain the necessity of war. The rush to war is the rush for peace. And we need more wars to suppress the coming of end times: the apocalypse versus the apocalypse; an eye for an eye; a tooth for a tooth. But also, we need more peace, the war of peace. There the apocalypse is stalled in the continuing present in order to prevent the real end.

FOURTH THESIS

Enter the anthropo(s) cene, the age of Man?[110] Or, was it the uncanny? How is Man, hitherto defined as animal rationale, getting into the scene as the return of the repressed?

104 John Sallis, *Chorology: On Beginning in Plato's Timaeus* (Bloomington and Indianapolis: Indiana University Press, 1999), 123.

105 We are referring here to the Aristotelian notion of unmoved mover.

106 Heidegger, *The Question Concerning Technology*, 34.

107 See Carl Schmitt, *The Nomos of the Earth in the International law of the*

Jus Publicum Europaeum, trans. G.L. Ulmen (New York: Telos Press Publishing, 2006). See also Raphael Gross, *Carl Schmitt and the Jews. The Jewish Question, the Holocaust, and German Legal Theory*, trans. Joel Golb (Madison: University of Wisconsin Press, 2007).

108 See Jacques Derrida, *The Specters of Marx: The State of the Debt, the Work of Mourning, and the New International* (New York: Routledge, 1994), 174.

109 Anneleen Masschelein, *Unconcept: The Freudian Uncanny in Late-Twentieth Century Theory* (Albany: State University of New York Press, 2011), 139.

110 Paul Crutzen and Eugene Stoermer, "The Anthropocene," *Global Change Newsletter*, 41 (2000): 17-18.

What is the nature of the scene, place or topos upon which this return will take place? On hindsight, Aristotle reduced the chora to a place or topos in his effort to unpack the errancy of this third kind into an objective-empirical presence.[111] Are we supposed to witness here the return of Man to the errancy of its causality? And yet insofar as it is in errancy, the place to return to will have to make a return journey of itself to its proper place as non-place, a-*topos*, albeit, reborn in ectopic pregnancy. Are we about to witness the return of Man by a self-negating process to the condition of possibility of a new event of creation, the chora? Something is about to happen to Man in the arrival of the anthropocene.

The anthropocene arrives in our midst with a curious unconcept, the nemesis for the non-place. In no other time a concept (the anthropocene) has become the avenger for the uncanny—the denial of conception's exceptional place in the heart of things. If a physicist has *six* numbers to describe the forces that shape the cosmos[112] we have a *ten* letter word, describing the unconcept,[113] which can undo the entire consistency of the human gaze, namely, extinction. Where it needs to be established that the true object of extinction is conception as "an assertive logic of presence,"[114] which is the real lesson of today's apocalypse, the human (as a principle) is here deprived of the function of the 'exceptional' with which it has hitherto identified its privilege as a species. There, the humanist trick goes from principle to organism. One could speak here of *destruktion* (sans its abusive Heideggerian connotation) as the logical stage of extinction discreetly propelling the historical transformation of this errant cause since the beginning of humanity's self-conception in mythos.

Here, where the legacy of Nietzsche should be emphasized, the uncanny persists as gay science, a wayward cause, an aesthetic contemplation without a goal, compared to the goal-oriented nihilism of the 'exceptional.' Curiously, in a kind of *détournement*, Nietzsche's model is the storytelling technique he borrowed from Plato which lies at the base of his aberrant type of rationalism. Though a similar kind of goal-orientation might have been Plato's tendency—in terms of binding the present to the proper recollection of the Forms, or the ideal world that could be mistaken for the goal itself—recollection was nonetheless proposed in view of addressing the present corruption of the polis. But *anamnesis* was never even planned in advance. The *Republic's* dialogue about the ideal form of government was not preconceived by any of the characters of Plato; rather, it was brought about by Plato's delirious use of storytelling.

Deleuze's interpretation of Plato is a crucial intervention at this point, sans the perversity of his too-modern injunction to create which is not even sufficiently nonhuman for which we should all be saying goodbye to conception. Whereas others see an *arch*-idealist, Deleuze sees in Plato "his own flights of intoxication,"[115] a raw inebriating presence,"[116] which speaks rather uncannily of his concealed, albeit genuine, metaphysical strength. And where it should also be established that Deleuze is a partisan of Nietzsche whose intoxication with Plato would have been too radical to a fault (Plato is both a cure and a poison, a *pharmakon* to gay science) had he not discovered for himself the restrained intoxication of the Forms, a counter-apocalypse to the exceptionality of Man in need of foundation[117] would have long ceased to attract its unfashionable defenders. In Deleuze's view of Plato's aim in the *Republic*, which is to "[construct] a model according to which the different pretenders can be judged,"[118] Plato can be considered offering a foundational political critique of hypocrisy.

The anthropocene arrives in our midst with a curious unconcept, the nemesis for the non-place. In no other time a concept (the anthropocene) has become the avenger for the uncanny—the denial of conception's exceptional place in the heart of things.

111   Alejandro A. Vallega, *Heidegger on the Issue of Space: Thinking on Exilic Grounds* (University Park Pennsylvania: The Pennsylvania State University, 2003), 41.

112   Martin Rees, *Just Six Numbers: The Deep Forces that Shape the Universe* (London: Phoenix, 2000).

113   Masschelein, *Unconcept*, 11.

114   Vallega, *Heidegger on the Issue of Space*, 41.

115   See Gregory Flaxman, ""Plato," in *Deleuze's Philosophical Lineage*, ed. Graham Hones and John Roffe (Edinburg: Edinburgh University Press, 2009), 13.

116   Gilles Deleuze, *Difference and Repetition*, trans. Paul Patton (London: Athlone Press, 1994), 59.

117   Gilles Deleuze, *Logic of Sense*, translated by Marx Lester (London: Athlone Press, 1990), 255

118   Deleuze, *Difference and Repetition*, 59.

FIFTH THESIS

In recent years, Francois Laruelle has been convincing us to expand this critique to an immanent criticism of philosophy by unmasking how it claims to see everything by its familiar gesture—the "look in the eye."[119] Laruelle would have us apprehend in this gesture what it actually means: "To look in the eye means: The Same is the eye and the eye—the matrix of speculation."[120] With seeing and conception at his disposal, the philosopher, in whose words Man is reduced to animal rationale, would have prior to the formal reduction "[looked] Man in the eye to dissolve the World into man and man into nothingness."[121] The rational animal is the full complement of this nothingness, an outcome of a malicious operation, of a self-seeing speculation of the Same; in short, a *hallucination*.

But Man—who can see prior to everything, as Laruelle would have us expand the intuition—is neither the rational animal (the barest of all concepts) nor the barest conception of existence in Dasein whose estrangement from the "Man' in Man-in-man,[122] the irreducible in the reduction of animal rationale, reveals its poorest intuition. Heidegger aims at the wrong Man, or rather, he seeks out the right Man, that of classical humanism and its much developed form in the metaphysic of subjectivity so as to identify its affordances to the destiny of nihilism in objective, technical reason; now a destiny that compels. Can we not have instead a 'Man' willing to "assign a question mark" to this suddenly revealed destiny?[123]

Writing in the wake of Aristotle, who is said to have quickly abandoned his speculation that there must be some-thing for man that corresponds to the idea of man without work or content, Agamben approaches a similar notion of irreducibility that brings this rational animal to the limits of its concept—namely, the "essential inoperativity of man."[124] The idea of man without vocation, without activity, is thinkable for the reductionist of Plato (Aristotle), and yet as it retreats deeply into the very heart of his unattested causality, it has to be abandoned in favor of objective presence according to which man is assigned his "proper nature." [125]

But, after centuries of being made to settle in "being-in-work,"[126] and in the whole history of production up till now, which means the reducibility of being to work, the irreducible remainder—what is made to settle there by the definition of man as animal rationale—has now become available for extraction, one for which Tiqqun, in a recent manifesto, would give the description readiness for civil war. [127]

Our task today is thus to heighten the civil war against this imperial definition of Man

Tiqqun's civil war mobilizes this remainder: a non-essential man, an impermanent non-man essence of the irreducible; a child-monster born of ectopic pregnancy, of the chorology of incest in the likeness of which we can figure out what is meant by Tiqqun's "[concept that cracks]" the ice in order to attain, and give rise, to experience."[128] Tiqqun's civil war is arguably the errant necessity that "makes ourselves handle [experience],"[129] that which makes us handle our own civil war, for instance, against the mighty academia, the empyreal ecology of explaining the object—this bastard concept—away in the inoculating system of reason.

On many times, since the great reduction of the irreducible some 2,000 years ago, this system has proven itself effective, especially when the great mass, including the laboring class of Marx, as Tiqqun observes, has come to "treat concepts with respect," [130] whose equivalent would be the resurgence of hallelujahs, or any sound pertinent to the nihilism of the will for which concepts become revered in place of the unattainable god.

---

119   See Francois Laruelle, "The Biography of the Eye," trans. Taylor Adkins, Fractal Ontology, entry posted on November 21, 2009, http://fractalontology.wordpress.com/2009/11/21/new-translations-of-laruelles-biography-of-the-eye. (Accessed November 24, 2014).

120   Ibid.

121   Ibid.

122   According to Laruelle, 'Man-in-man" is what makes humans human. It is also meant in Laruelle's vocabulary as the point at which humans "cease to be anonymous transcendentals and indicates the reduction which makes them humans" (See Anthony Paul Smith, "Glossary Raisonné: Rules for Writing Non-Philosophy (Vocabulary and Syntax)," in Francois Laruelle, *Future Christ: A Lesson in Heresy*, trans. Anthony Paul Smith [London and New York: Continuum, 2010], xxvii). In the history of philosophy, the reduction of the human is achieved by defining it as animal rationale. Our point here is that the 'Man' in 'Man-in-man' is what remains irreducible in the reduction of this founding act of humanism.

123   Cf. n. 97.

---

124   Giorgio Agamben, "What is a destituent power," *Environment and Planning D: Society and Space*, 32 (2014): 69.

125   Ibid.

126   Agamben, "What is a destituent power," 73.

127   See Tiqqun, *Introduction to Civil War*, trans. Alexander Galloway and Jason E. Smith (Los Angeles, California: Semiotext(e), 2010).

128   Ibid., 12.

129   Ibid.

130   Ibid., 75; See also Friedrich Nietzsche, *Gay Science*, trans. Josefine Nauckhoff (Cambridge: Cambridge University Press, 2001), 128.

Our task today is thus to heighten the civil war against this imperial definition of Man by refusing its work, to render its work destitute, in favor of the impotentiality of the delirium, of being-outside-work, outside the economic rule of reason.

SIXTH THESIS

Bent to expose the pretension of intelligence or conception at its highest point, the Platonic delirium is the very defining essence of the chora. And isn't humanity, the Man-in-man, this destituent power, the true heir to chora whose very indefinability points to the fact that we were never rational animals to begin with? As a logical principle of causation, this rational animal must be thrown away for good. What should go extinct is this in/human principle. Nietzsche's declaration, that 'the human is a disease that must be overcome,'[131] should have blasted our ears long ago in mythic proportions.

It is in this light that Agamben offers a kind of recovery. For those aspiring, "it is necessary … first to release oneself from the form that [it has] received in the exception,"[132] the exception being the operability of the state of utter nudity of man in animal rationale, its bareness under the stripping power of reason and its light. With destituent power, this exception will also have to recover its life: it too has a life despite its negating function, but precisely because it will recover its true formerity that it must be seen recovering as a pretention. It shall then be its revelation out of hiding, the true apocalypse.

But how, one may ask, can the exceptional ever self-immolate on our behalf? It may be in light of this question that the question is perverse, in the sense that it gives content (quite unknowingly but just the same satisfies the unconscious of the work), to the being that the question itself presupposes, namely, the being-exceptional. Nothing is more perverse than the speed with which thought affords work to this being—it is work, whose origin conceals itself in potentiality in a manner that no one can suspect, thus the speed which veils in advance a consciousness already veiled by work, to which we must object the unattested care (*sorge*) of inoperability, a conscientious praxis. Why not instead guarantee in advance that there will be sufficient logistics for the self-immolation of the being-exceptional?

It certainly makes sense to save what fossil fuel is left of earth not only to open the economy of the remainder to the

suffering, once and for all, but also that the fuel may teach the fire to finally touch and burn the cotton. As the saying goes, 'it is not fire that burns the cotton, but god,' which is actually the same as to say, it is not the economy that burns the skin, already exposed to the measure of the exception, but a higher principle. To expose the academia that encourages this form of thinking to the measure of the irreducible is one thing; to expose it to fire is another. Only in the silence of this preparation can we speak of a true political theology.

To the nihilism of the exceptional which still persists—its systematic continuity in the historical reductionisms of the apocalypse, pitting one apocalypse against another so that the real one is infinitely delayed (or, should we all be thinking that the anthropocene is the new katechon of our age, a critical form of reason simply playing out its guilt to achieve catharsis at the same time that it suppresses the unattested idiolect of our age?)—we offer a timely response with which we wish to conclude and which comes to this point with a bit of recollecting that "once upon a time:"

There was a creature that came out of the darkness with only a faint memory of water, and sand, and fear to discover that its very life depended on telling a story about its origins—of which it had no clear memory, and its destiny—of which it had no clear knowledge… [Neither] Ape nor Angel, it remains a creature caught between, looking through a fractured mirror at possibilities always just beyond reach. It is a changeling creature, a child seeming stolen from the gods.[133]

Virgilio Rivas

is currently affiliated to the Polytechnic University of the Philippines, a state university in the Philippines touted sparingly as a 'poor man's university' in this part of the region (Southeast Asia). He teaches philosophy, and chairs the Department of Philosophy and Humanities and the Theater Arts Department.

---

131   See Friedrich Nietzsche. *Thus Spoke Zarathustra. A Book for All and None*, trans. Adrian Del Caro (Cambridge: Cambridge University Press, 2006).

132   Agamben, "What is a destituent power," 73.

133   Quoted from Lawrence Kimmel, "The Mythic Journey of A Changeling," in *Existence, Historical Fabulation, Destiny*, ed. Anna-Teresa Tymieniecka (The Netherlands: Springer, 2009), 11.

Natural Habitat
(Nimue Brown)

Urban is not a place, not truly
But a state of being, unaware
Narrow vision of fabrication
Sees only what it expects.
Urban the view of brick and car
Eyes for tarmac, concrete, glass.

For the fox, no separation.
Garden, wasteland, woodland.
Hard or soft under paws
All places to be alive
Canal otter, peregrine nesting
On the old coms tower.

No separation – bats moth-hunting still
Beneath street light glow.
Urban is inside you, an illusion
For there is always sky above
Always sun wind rain air breath.
Always blood and digestion.

Small bird at your window ledge
Moss tenacious in cracks
Day and night, and day again
In all the seasons.
How carefully you must avoid
Life, nature, truth.

Gaze into the headlights, focus
On humanity's creative powers.
Just another tiny ant
Upon the ancient ant hill
Who refuses to look up
And admit there is a sky.

Nimue Brown
Nimue Brown is the author of assorted Pagan
non-fiction texts published by Moon Books,
an array of eccentric fiction and a blog –
www.druidlife.wordpress.com.

An Apparently Impossible Problem

A Winter's Tale
(Rhyd Wildermuth)

Extinction. Climate change. War. Dying oceans, dying forests. The earth shattered beneath us to get at the last bits of hydrocarbons and water. Food shortages. Refugees fleeing fighting, poverty, poison, religious feuds.

Capitalism and its physical manifestation—industrialisation—have so thoroughly transformed our environment, our social relations, our imaginations that the very idea of throwing off this system and having another—one where we humans live in community with everything else which shares this planet—seems to be an apparently impossible problem.

I know. I'm sorry.

But I also know something about apparently impossible problems. Mind if I tell you a story?

There was this moment with a lover of mine, a few winters ago. We'd gone together to get wax to make candles and the stuff for glühwein (German mulled wine), and we got stuck on a bus in a snowstorm at the bottom of a steep hill. We'd had little time to do much together, had both been ground-down by our jobs and the difficulties of our relationship and our various lives, and this simple errand had been a beautiful thing to do together, seemingly crushed by a sudden storm.

The bus wasn't going anywhere. Cars spun out, slid back down the hill past the bus. We were gonna be there for hours before the bus would ever start moving again, and it looked like the world was against us, the same way every awesome thing we– both from abject poverty and families rife with mental troubles–ever tried to do would fall apart in the face of impossibility.

Both of our lives, actually, were impossible. I grew up in abject poverty in Appalachia to an abusive father and a developmentally-disabled (they used to call people with her intelligence quotient "retarded") mother who later developed schizophrenia His mother? Addicted to drugs since he was a child. He'd tell me a story about being 14 and being left with his 6-month old half-brother for days on end, trying to figure out what to do with a baby while his mother was out drug-seeking. I'd tell him stories of being in South Florida trying to raise my sisters and pay rent at 14 while my divorced and schizophrenic mother talked back to voices telling her to drive my sisters and I off a bridge into the water. And it's funny, because he and I would have arguments about whose childhood was harder (I thought his, he thought mine).

The world's a fucking impossible place, and we both knew this a little better than most.

And we're sitting there in this bus as the snow falls and cars slide past us, hitting each other in the great chaos of human effort against nature. That bus wasn't fucking going anywhere, but you know what we did?

We got off the bus and walked.

Trudging up that icy hill in a snowstorm, laughing, watching all the silly people in their silly cars trying to get up that hill, catching snowflakes on our tongues, pushing stuck cars on our way up...the impossible is always impossible only if you insist on going on precisely the way you think you're supposed to.

If we can't have cars and mass-produced shit and 40-hour work weeks in lifeless jobs without ruining the planet, we can just start walking and making stuff that lasts and working less in more meaningful ways.

If we can't have smartphones and computer games and 400 television channels and fresh strawberries in winter, then we can write letters and play cards and tell stories and make strawberry jam in the summer.

If we can't make absurd amounts of money off of selling houses and derivatives and weight-loss programs and plastic toys, then we make absurd amounts of joy and equality in societies where people grow gardens and tend forests and no one gets to ruin other people's lives on account of having more money than others.

So what if that bus isn't getting up the hill in the snowstorm? We can walk up the hill and catch snowflakes on our tongues and warm our winter-chilled bodies with each others' flesh when we get to the top.

The way past the impossible usually just involves giving up some certainty that is keeping you on a snow-bound bus at the bottom of a hill, some habit, some reliance on an expectation that isn't serving you any longer.

You can carry a rucksack full of wax and wine up a snowy hill with your lover and laugh and make mulled wine and warm yourself and each other with the love falling like rain and snow from the skies. You can read by the light of burning barricades and plant chamomile in the cracked pavement and tell stories of what it was like when we thought we should ignore the gods and the dead.

We can side with the poor and the streams and forests and crows and the forgotten, because there's so many of us, you know, and we have the best stories.

And we can start building now. Actually, **we must.** If we're to counter their violence with something other than violence, *a game we can never win*, we must create the world we want now. A world full of gods, a world of remembered dead, a world others want to join and help create, one that doesn't flood the cities and poison the waters and raze the forests and abuse women or favor one skin color over all others.

The first step's easy.

You just have to leave the stuck bus, and make sure you help others up the hill on your way.

Rhyd Wildermuth

often lives in a city by the Salish Sea in occupied Duwamish territory. He's a bard, theorist, anarchist, and writer, the editor of A Beautiful Resistance and co-founder of Gods&Radicals, author of Your Face Is a Forest and a columnist for The Wild Hunt. He growls when he's thinking, laughs when he's happy, cries when he's sad, and does all those things when he's in love. He worships Welsh gods, drinks a lot of tea, and dreams of forests, revolution, and men. His words can be found at Paganarch.com

Aaron Shenewolf

Photographs: 20, 26, 32, 61, 90, 102

Born and raised at the feet of the might Cascade Mountains, Aaron Shenewolf is an artist, photographer, and student of cultural anthropology. Amateur dreamer and self-proclaimed dharma bum, he's prone to flights of fancy and falls in love with every country, city, mountain or stream he encounters. Founder of Over The Moon Photographie, his work depicts the landscapes and cityscapes of the great wildernesses of America:
flickr.com/photos/jumping-luna

Wespennest

(Photographs: 41, 50, 108)

A freelance photojournalist, my professional area of interest and expertise is documenting protests and exposing hate groups. The level of intensity that such work demands can be overtaxing, so I find strength and solace in nature, which I find to be more supernatural than mundane. It is no great stretch to see a strong link between resistance to capitalism and paganism, as most strains of paganism are diametrically opposed to the typical excesses that comprise capitalist normalcy. Further, it becomes more plain for me to see a mutually beneficial relationship between the capitalist ruling classes and racist hate groups-- keep the working classes divided over arbitrary values (like the amount of melanin in one person's body) and they will be more reluctant to unite against the capitalist power structure. Deny these shadowy hate groups the ability to organize in secret and a key element of societal control is significantly weakened. How to do this is as varied as the threat it confronts, and the astral plane is no less of a battlefield than the street. Multiple gods, no masters! Find his work at
flickr.com/photos/wespennest

Loïs Cordelia ASGFA

(Gaze of the Green Man, page 96)

(born 1982, Ipswich) is a prolific UK artist and illustrator in cut-paper, acrylics and mixed media. She works in diverse styles, ranging from intricate scalpel paper-cut designs to energetic acrylic speed-painting. Since 1999, she has been a studio assistant to children's illustrator Jan Pienkowski (born 1936, Warsaw), and holds a first level Honours degree in Arabic from the University of Edinburgh. Loïs' website includes a comprehensive portfolio and a dynamic record of her busy schedule of exhibitions, live art demos, workshops, talks, and other events.
www.LoisCordelia.com

Li Pallas

(Cover Design)

is a neon sentimentalist who invents environments about the incorrigibility of love and belonging. An artist/designer + critical theorist living and working in Los Angeles, California. Recurrent debates with her magnum cum laude economist stepfather prepped her to navigate and discuss the nuances of the political economy, and she is carving out a life where she can express these thoughts in print media and printed matter. She is available for hire for print and web design, organizational strategizing, facilitation, and general analytics. She also enjoys neuroscience. Find her work at:
LiPallasLovesYou.com

Works Cited

FINCHUILL, BECOMING PLACED

American Heritage Dictionary of Indo-European Roots, The. 3rd. Ed. by Calvert Watkins.

    Boston: Houghton Mifflin Harcourt, 2011.

Bacon, Francis. *New Atlantis*. Montana: Kessinger.

Berman, Morris. *The Reenchantment of the World*. NY: Bantam, 1984.

Casey, Edward S. *The Fate of Place: A Philosophical History*. Berkeley: University of

    California Press, 1997.

--. *Getting Back Into Place: Toward A Renewed Understanding Of The Place-World*. 2nd Ed. Indiana: Indiana UP, 2009.

Haraway, Donna. *Modest_Witness @ Second_Millennium.Female Man Meets OncoMouse: Feminism and Technoscience*. New York: Routledge, 1997.

Harvey, Graham. *Animism: Respecting The Living World*. New York: Columbia, 2006.

Lincoln, Bruce. *Theorizing Myth: Narrative, Ideology, And Scholarship*. Chicago: U of

    Chicago Press, 2000.

Merchant, Carolyn. *The Death of Nature: Women, Ecology and the Scientific Revolution*.

    San Francisco: HarperCollins. 1980.

Oxford Dictionary of English Etymology. Ed. C.T. Onions. Oxford: Oxford UP, 1966.

Sepúlveda, Jesús. *The Garden of Particularities*. Los Angeles: Feral House, 2005.

Weber, Max. *The Protestant Ethic And The Spirit Of Capitalism*. London: Routledge,

    1992 (original 1930).

Uncivilized: The Best of Green Anarchy. Eugene: 2012.

JONATHAN WOOLLEY—THE MATTER OF THE GODS

Asad, T. (1993) Genealogies of Religion. Johns Hopkins Univ. Press: Baltimore.

Augustine, Saint – Bishop of Hippo (2014) De civitate Dei – English and Latin. Harvard University Press: Cambridge MA.

Beckett, J. (2014) The Four Centers of Paganism in Under the Ancient Oaks (Patheos). Available at http://www.patheos.com/blogs/johnbeckett/2014/05/the-four-centers-of-paganism.html. Last accessed on 13/09/2015.

Bridger, M. and Hergest, S. (1997) Pagan Deism: Three Views in The Pomegranate: The International Journal of Pagan Studies Vol. 1 No. 1 pp. 37-42.

Doyle-White, E. (2012) "In Defence of Pagan Studies: A Response to Davidsen's Critique" inThe Pomegranate: The International Journal of Pagan Studies, Vol. 14, No. 1, pp. 5-21.

Foucault, M. (1972) The Archaeology of Knowledge, trans. A. M. Sheridan Smith. Routledge: London.

Kushner, T. (2003) Angels in America. HBO: United States.

Luhrmann, T. (1989) Persuasions of the Witch's Craft: Ritual Magic in Contemporary England. Cambridge, Mass.: Harvard University Press.

Magliocco, S. (2013) Sabina Magliocco: Pagan Fundamentalism? In The Wild Hunt. Available at http://wildhunt.org/2013/02/sabina-magliocco-pagan-fundamentalism.html. Last accessed 13/09/2015.

Pratchett, T. (1991) Witches Abroad. Victor Gollancz: London.

HEATHEN CHINESE: ARE THE GODS ON OUR SIDE?

Duara, Prasenjit. "Superscribing Symbols: The Myth of Guandi, Chinese God of War." *The Journal of Asian Studies* 47.4 (1988): 778-795. Web.

Levin, Ned. "Hong Kong Protests: Guan Yu is the People's Deity: Protestors, Police and Triads Show Reverence for Chinese Deified General." *The Wall Street Journal*. 30 Oct. 2014. Web.

Lydon, Sandy. *Chinese Gold: The Chinese in the Monterey Bay Region*. Capitola: Capitola Book Co, 1985. Print

P. SUFENAS VIRIUS LUPUS: EARTH GODDESSES RISING

Finnchuill, "The Wind is Rising, " https://finchuillsmast.wordpress.com/20115/08/16/the-wind-is-rising/ (accessed October 12, 2015

Heathen Chinese, "Millenarianism, Pt. 2: The Yellow Turbans," https://heathenchinese.wordpress.com/2013/04/01/millenarianism-pt-2-the-yellow-turbans/ (Accessed October 12, 2015)

Hesiod, *Theogony, Works and Days, Shield*, trans. Apostolos N. Athanassakis (Baltimore and London: The Johns Hopkins University Press, 1983)

P. Sufenas Virius Lupus, "Demeter's Other Children: Demophoön and the Eleusinian Mysterieies," in Melitta Benu and Revecca Buchanan (eds)., *Potnia: A Devotional Anthology in Honor of Demeter* (Asheville, NC: Bibliotheca Alexandrina, 2014), pp. 190-198

P. Sufenas Virius Lupus,, "The Lack of Greek Eschatalogy," https://aediculaantinoi.wordpress.com/2014/07/26/the-lack-of-greek-eschatology/ (accessed October 12, 2015)

A.T. Murray (ed/trans), *Homer, Illiad*, revised by Murray F. Wyatt, 2 volumes (Cambridge: Harvard University Press, 1922)

Maurice Platnauer (ed./trans.), *Claudian, Volume II* (CambridgeL Harvard University Press, 1922)

Alan Richardson, Earth God Rising: The Return of the Male Mysteries (St. Paun, MN: Llewellyn Publications, 1990).

Rhyd Wildermuth, "Dahut at the Floodgate," http://paganarch.com/2015/08/16/dahut-at-the-floodgate/ (accessed October 12, 2015

ANTHONY RELLA: THE SOUL IS A SITE OF LIBERATION

Foa, E.; Hembree, E. & Rothbaum, B.O. (2007). Prolonged exposure therapy for PTSD: Emotional processing of traumatic experiences. New York, NY: Oxford University Press.

Norcross, J. & Lambert, M. (2010). Evidence-based therapy relationships. Substance Abuse and Mental Health Service Administration. http://www.nrepp.samhsa.gov/pdfs/Norcross_evidence-based_therapy_relationships.pdf

Morris, D. (2015). Trauma post trauma. Slate.com

FJOTHR LOKAKVAN: LIFE SUPPORT SYSTEMS

Lessing, Doris: Prison We Choose to Live Inside, Harper and Row, Publishers, Inc., 1987

Edwards, Michael, "To remain in prison for the rest of my life is the greatest honor you could give me: the story of Sister Megan Rice," openDemocracy.net, 2014

Oliver, Mary, Dream Work, Atlantic Monthly Press, 1986

VIRGILIO RIVAS: A COUNTER-APOCALYPSE FOR OUR TIME

Agamben, Giorgio. "What is a destituent power," *Environment and Planning D: Society and Space*, 32 (2014): 65-74.

Aristotle. "Physics: Book IV." In *The Complete Works of Aristotle*. Edited by Jonathan Barnes. Princeton, New Jersey: Princeton University Press, 1991.

Callahan, Allen Dwight. "The Language of the Apocalypse." *The Harvard Theological Review*, Vol. 88 4 (October 1995): 453-470.

Crutzen, Paul and Eugene Stoermer. "The Anthropocene." *Global Change Newsletter*, 41 (2000): 17-18.

Deleuze, Gilles. *Logic of Sense*. Translated by Marx Lester. London: Athlone Press, 1990.

___. *Difference and Repetition*. Translated by Paul Patton. London: Athlone Press, 1994.

Deleuze, Gilles and Claire Parnet. *Dialogues*. Translated by Hugh Tomlinson. New York: Columbia University Press, 1987.

Derrida, Jacques. *The Specters of Marx: The State of the Debt, the Work of Mourning, and the New International*. New York: Routledge, 1994.

Epstein, Mark. *Going to Pieces Without Falling Apart: A Buddhist Perspective on Wholeness*. New York: Broadway Books, 1999.

Flaxman, Gregory. "Plato." In *Deleuze's Philosophical Lineage*. Edited by Graham Hones and John Roffe. Edinburg: Edinburgh University Press, 2009.

Gross, Raphael. *Carl Schmitt and the Jews. The Jewish Question, the Holocaust, and German Legal Theory*. Translated by Joel Golb. Madison: University of Wisconsin Press, 2007.

Heidegger, Martin. *Being and Time*. Translated by John Macquarrie and Edward Robinson. Oxford: Basil Blackwell, 1962.

___. *The Question Concerning Technology and Other Essays*. Translated by William Lovitt. New York and London: Garland Publishing, Inc., 1977.

___. *Basic Writings of Martin Heidegger*. Translated and Edited by David Farrell Krell. London: Routledge, 1993.

___. *Contributions to Philosophy: From Enowning*. Translated by Parvis Emad and Kenneth Maly. Bloomington and Indianapolis: Indiana University Press, 1999.

Hesiod. "Theogony." In *The Homeric Hymns and Homerica*. Translated by Hugh G. Evelyn-White. Edited by. G.P. Goold. Cambridge, Massachusetts: Harvard University Press, 1982.

Janicaud, Dominique. *Heidegger from Metaphysics to Thought*. Translated by Michael Gendre. Albany: State University of New York Press, 1995.

Kimmel, Lawrence. "The Mythic Journey of A Changeling," in *Existence, Historical Fabulation, Destiny*, ed. Anna-Teresa Tymieniecka. The Netherlands: Springer, 2009

Laruelle, Francois. *Future Christ: A Lesson in Heresy*. Translated by Anthony Paul Smith. London and New York: Continuum, 2010.

___. "The Biography of the Eye." Translated by Taylor Adkins, Fractal Ontology, entry posted on November 21, 2009, http://fractalontology.wordpress.com/2009/11/21/new-translations-of-laruelles-biography-of-the-eye (Accessed November 24, 2014).

Masschelein, Anneleen. *Unconcept: The Freudian Uncanny in Late-Twentieth Century Theory*. Albany: State University of New York Press, 2011.

Mathewson, David L. *Verbal Aspect in the Book of Revelation: The Function of Greek Verb Tenses in John's Apocalypse*. Leiden, Boston: Brill, 2010.

Meillassoux, Quentin. *The Number and the Siren. A Decipherment of Mallarmé's Coup de Dés*. Translated by Robin Mackay. United Kingdom: Urbanomic Press, 2012.

___. *After Finitude. An Essay on the Necessity of Contingency*. Translated by Brassier. London: Continuum, 2008.

Middleton, Christopher. (Ed. and Trans.). *Selected Letters of Friedrich Nietzsche* (Chicago: Chicago University Press, 1969.

Nietzsche, Friedrich. *Gay Science*. Translated by Josefine Nauckhoff. Cambridge: Cambridge University Press, 2001.

___. *Thus Spoke Zarathustra. A Book for All and None*. Translated by Adrian Del Caro. Cambridge: Cambridge University Press, 2006.

Plato. *Plato: Timaeus and Critias*. Translated by Robin Waterfield. Oxford: Oxford University Press, 2008.

Rees, Martin. *Just Six Numbers: The Deep Forces that Shape the Universe*. London: Phoenix, 2000.

Rinella, Michael A. *Pharmakon: Plato, Drug Culture, and Identity in Ancient Athens*. United Kingdom: Lexington Books, 2010.

Sallis, John. *Chorology: On Beginning in Plato's Timaeus*. Bloomington and Indianapolis: Indiana University Press, 1999.

Schmitt, Carl. *The Nomos of the Earth in the International law of the Jus Publicum Europaeum*. Translated by G.L. Ulmen. New York: Telos Press Publishing, 2006.

Tiqqun. *Introduction to Civil War*. Translated by Alexander Galloway and Jason E. Smith. Los Angeles, California: Semiotext(e), 2010.

Vallega, Alejandro. *Heidegger on the Issue of Space: Thinking on Exilic Grounds*. University Park Pennsylvania: The Pennsylvania State University, 2003.

CPSIA information can be obtained
at www.ICGtesting.com
Printed in the USA
LVOW01s1439131115

462412LV00007B/14/P